Multiple Intelligences
in the
Mathematics Classroom

Hope Martin

This Book Purchased From

Alps Publishing
P.O. Box 2264 Greeley, CO 80632
(970) 330-2577 (800) 345-2577 Fax (970) 330-2391

Other multiple intelligences books published by IRI/Skylight Training and Publishing:

If the Shoe Fits . . . : How to Develop Multiple Intelligences in the Classroom
by Carolyn Chapman

Integrating Curricula with Multiple Intelligences: Teams, Themes, and Threads
by Robin Fogarty and Judy Stoehr

Multiple Assessments for Multiple Intelligences
by James Bellanca, Carolyn Chapman, and Elizabeth Swartz

Multiple Intelligences: A Collection
Robin Fogarty and James Bellanca, editors

A Multiple Intelligences Road to a Quality Classroom
by Sally Berman

Seven Pathways of Learning: Teaching Students and Parents about Multiple Intelligences
by David Lazear

Seven Ways of Teaching: The Artistry of Teaching with Multiple Intelligences
by David Lazear

Seven Windows to a Child's World: 100 Ideas for the Multiple Intelligences Classroom
by Anna T. O'Connor and Sheila Callahan-Young

Multiple Intelligences in the Mathematics Classroom

Published by IRI/SkyLight Training and Publishing, Inc.
2626 South Clearbrook Drive, Arlington Heights, IL 60005
800-348-4474 or 847-290-6600
Fax 847-290-6609
info@iriskylight.com
http://www.iriskylight.com

Creative Director: Robin Fogarty
Managing Editor: Julia E. Noblitt
Editor: Monica Phillips
Proofreader: Troy Slocum
Graphic Designer: Heidi Ray
Cover and Illustration Designer: David Stockman
Production Supervisor: Bob Crump

LCCCN 95-81187
ISBN 1-57517-010-8

1672D-1-98 McN
Item number 1421
06 05 04 03 02 01 99 98   15 14 13 12 11 10 9 8 7 6 5 4

*This book is dedicated to all of the people
who, over the years, have apologetically said,
"Math was always my worst subject; I was
always terrible in math." This book is for you!*

Acknowledgments

My thanks go out to the thousands of students who, during these past twenty-five years, have lived through the metamorphosis of my teaching philosophy and have helped me hone my craft.

I have also had the privilege during my career of working with a number of administrators who encouraged my experimentation and contributed to my maturation. The following three administrators played a particularly important role in bringing me to where I am today, philosophically.

Dr. Oliver McCracken took a chance and hired me for my first teaching job. By sharing his remarkable work ethic and vast experience, Olie taught me that successful teachers work hard to meet the needs of their students, remembering that they teach children, not subjects.

Three children and twelve years later, I had the opportunity to work with Ron Finotti, a principal who encouraged me to attend state and national math conferences, to expand my knowledge and enlarge my repertoire of classroom strategies. Regardless of the financial problems of the district, Ron always found the money for staff development!

An extra big "thank you" goes to Griff Powell, a very talented superintendent who encouraged me to share my ideas with my colleagues and teach them what I had learned over the years.

Finally, I would like to thank all of the teachers who have attended my workshops and sat through my classes. Whenever I work with teachers, knowledge flows both ways. By sharing their insights and experiences, they have helped me sharpen and solidify my beliefs.

Contents

Chart of NCTM Standards

	Algebra	Computation and Estimation	Geometry	Mathematical Connections	Mathematics as Communication	Mathematics as Problem Solving	Mathematics as Reasoning	Measurement	Number and Number Relationships	Number Systems and Theory	Patterns and Functions	Statistics/ Probability
$1,000,000 Long		●	●	●	●	●	●	●	●	●		●
How Many Strides to Walk around the Earth?		●		●	●	●	●	●	●			●
Patterns in the 100s Chart				●	●	●	●		●	●	●	
Rectangles and Factors		●	●	●	●	●	●		●	●	●	
Venn Diagrams: LCM and GCF	●	●		●	●	●	●		●	●		
Folding a Tangram		●	●	●	●	●	●	●				
Making a Tangram Quilt		●	●	●	●	●	●	●		●		
Dessert for a Crowd		●		●	●	●	●		●	●		
5 x 5 Puzzle Cents	●	●		●	●	●	●		●	●		
Chocolate Chip Cookies		●		●	●	●	●		●	●		
Music and Fractions		●		●	●	●	●		●	●		
Mathematical Palindromes		●		●	●	●	●		●		●	●
Pentominoes			●	●	●	●	●	●				
Open-Top Boxes	●	●	●	●	●	●	●	●	●		●	●
Classifying Polygons	●		●	●	●	●	●					
Explorations with Cereal Boxes		●	●	●	●	●	●	●				
Designing Cereal Boxes		●	●	●	●	●	●	●				
The Painted Cube	●	●	●	●	●	●	●	●		●	●	●

(Continued on next page)

Chart of NCTM Standards (Continued)

	Algebra	Computation and Estimation	Geometry	Mathematical Connections	Mathematics as Communication	Mathematics as Problem Solving	Mathematics as Reasoning	Measurement	Number and Number Relationships	Number Systems and Theory	Patterns and Functions	Statistics/ Probability
Cubes That Grow	●	●	●	●	●	●	●				●	
Just How Big Is the Statue of Liberty?		●		●	●	●	●	●	●			●
Gummi Worms		●		●	●	●	●					●
How Long Is Your Digestive System?		●		●	●	●	●					●
What Happened 1,000,000 Seconds Ago?		●		●	●	●	●		●			
How Long Would It Take to Walk to China?	●	●	●	●	●	●	●		●		●	●
Buying Apples by the Pound		●		●	●	●	●		●	●		●
EggsCetera		●	●	●	●	●	●		●	●		●
Super Survey		●		●	●	●	●			●		●
What Is Your Favorite Subject?		●		●	●	●	●			●	●	●
One Die and Probability		●		●	●	●	●		●	●	●	●
Pair of Dice and Probability		●		●	●	●	●		●	●		●
Is This Game Fair?		●		●	●	●	●		●	●		●
Dinosaurs and Probability		●		●	●	●	●		●	●		●

Chart of Intelligences

	Verbal/Linguistic	Musical/Rhythmic	Logical/Mathematical	Visual/Spatial	Bodily/Kinesthetic	Interpersonal	Intrapersonal	Naturalist
$1,000,000 Long	●		●	●	●	●	●	
How Many Strides to Walk around the Earth?	●		●	●	●	●	●	
Patterns in the 100s Chart	●		●	●				●
Rectangles and Factors	●		●	●		●		
Venn Diagrams: LCM and GCF			●	●		●		
Folding a Tangram	●		●	●	●		●	
Making a Tangram Quilt	●		●	●		●		
Dessert for a Crowd	●		●			●		
5 x 5 Puzzle Cents	●		●		●		●	
Chocolate Chip Cookies	●		●			●		
Music and Fractions	●	●	●			●		
Mathematical Palindromes	●	●	●			●		
Pentominoes	●		●	●	●	●		
Open-Top Boxes	●		●	●	●	●		
Classifying Polygons	●		●	●			●	●
Explorations with Cereal Boxes	●		●	●	●	●		
Designing Cereal Boxes	●		●	●	●	●	●	
The Painted Cube	●		●	●	●	●	●	

(Continued on next page)

Chart of Intelligences *(Continued)*

	Verbal/ Linguistic	Musical/ Rhythmic	Logical/ Mathematical	Visual/ Spatial	Bodily/ Kinesthetic	Interpersonal	Intrapersonal	Naturalist
Cubes That Grow	●		●	●		●		
Just How Big Is the Statue of Liberty?	●		●	●	●	●	●	
Gummi Worms	●		●	●	●		●	●
How Long Is Your Digestive System?	●		●		●	●	●	
What Happened 1,000,000 Seconds Ago?	●		●			●		
How Long Would It Take to Walk to China?	●		●	●	●	●		
Buying Apples by the Pound			●	●	●	●		
EggsCetera	●		●	●	●	●		●
Super Survey	●		●	●		●		
What Is Your Favorite Subject?	●		●	●		●	●	●
One Die and Probability	●		●	●	●	●		
Pair of Dice and Probability	●		●	●	●	●		
Is This Game Fair?	●		●	●	●	●	●	
Dinosaurs and Probability	●		●	●	●	●		

Foreword

Hope Martin has answered a need for me and all teachers of mathematics by giving a sensible way to put multiple intelligences in the mathematics curriculum. A sensible approach for another look at how students conceive and use mathematics.

Assessment in mathematics is a real problem for many teachers because most assessments are not suited to what students should learn. Hope Martin gives new insight into the assessment situation with very simple explanations and good examples. The grading matrix is the best approach to assessing problem solving that I have ever seen. The book gives examples of problems and clearly explains how to apply the grading matrix.

The last part of the book has a variety of lessons that can be used in the classroom. The "Making a Tangram Quilt" activity was a new lesson for me that the students enjoyed. Another one I tried was "Music and Fractions," which made learning fractions fun. There are many other lessons that every teacher will want to try.

I highly recommend *Multiple Intelligences in the Mathematics Classroom* to any teacher who wants a new look at the teaching of mathematics. This book will stimulate and educate you.

LOLA J. MAY

Introduction
It's Broken? Let's Fix It

Mathematics seems to be a stable, tradition-bound, and secure part of the curriculum, while everything else appears to change on a regular basis. Countries emerge and disappear, science theories are born and die, reading pedagogies go in and out of vogue, but math, in the traditional sense, endures. Or does it?

In many forty-five-minute classes, thirty minutes is spent reviewing the previous day's lesson, ten minutes on teaching new material, and the last five minutes on the students' working the problems. This type of classroom uses the "ABC" method of teaching mathematics: austere, boring, and colorless.

For more than three decades there have been calls to reform the way mathematics is taught and learned. Why? The needs of society have changed as the industrial age has given way to the information age. Moreover, our understanding of cognition and the needs of our students has increased enormously.

The impetus for change began back on October 4, 1957, when *Sputnik I* ("fellow traveler of Earth"), the first successful manmade satellite, was launched from the USSR. This was our first hint that something needed to be changed in the way math and science was being taught; thus began the examination of our educational system (once believed to be the best in the world). The world seemed to be changing while our beliefs remained static. In the next ten years, we saw the arrival and departure of "modern math," followed by the "back-to-basics" movement. These two mathematical pedagogies were at opposite ends of the philosophical spectrum, but both were reactions to America's awareness that some change was needed.

"Back to basics" had a stronghold until 1978, when the National Assessment of Educational Progress completed a survey that found students appeared to have a good grasp of arithmetic computational skills but could not use these skills to solve problems. Roy Forbes, the director of National Assessment, said:

> During a period when the public has placed a great emphasis on the "basics," assessment data shows that mathematics achievement has declined, especially in problem-solving and understanding of concepts. An expanded definition of what is "basic" in mathematics is needed so that students will be better equipped to deal with a variety of problems. (NAEP Newsletter 1979)

In the 1980s, the National Council of Teachers of Mathematics (NCTM) published *Agenda for Action,* which recommended that (1) problem solving be the focus of school mathematics, (2) the concept of what is a "basic skill" be expanded, (3) the use of calculators and computers be incorporated into the teaching of math, (4) more nontraditional assessments be used to evaluate student progress, and (5) the curriculum be examined to meet the diverse needs of students.

In 1989, the Mathematical Sciences Education Board published *Everybody Counts,* a document that raised serious concerns about the equity of mathematics education. The conception that mathematics served as a filter rather than a pump, filtering some of our students out of math-related careers and into lower-paying professions, made educators in this country sit up and take notice. The majority of students affected were women and minority students. Who or what was at fault? The Mathematical Sciences Education Board placed the blame on the entire system, from society's beliefs about who can learn and do math to the way mathematics is taught in our elementary, secondary, and college educational systems. *Everybody Counts* took a global view of the problem and led the way for calls for substantive changes from the NCTM.

THE EMERGENCE OF SUBSTANTIVE AND LASTING CHANGE

In 1989, the NCTM published the *Curriculum and Evaluation Standards for School Mathematics,* which delineates (1) why we should change, (2) how the change should occur, (3) what the mathematics curriculum should be for grades K–12, and (4) how to assess the progress of our students. This document has had a great impact on current changes in mathematics. It challenges outdated assumptions that mathematics is a fixed and unchanging body of knowledge and that to do mathematics we must calculate answers according to a specific rule or algorithm. The following are six of the reasons for change:

- We have moved into an age of information and technology where there is little use for "shopkeeper arithmetic."

- Technology should and must play a more important role in the classroom.

- The body of mathematical knowledge and its uses have grown as a result of technology.

- Changes have occurred in American society. (Society expects schools to help all students become mathematically literate).

- Mathematics must meet the needs of our global economy.

- Our knowledge of how students learn should become an integral part of our teaching strategies.

The NCTM standards encourage the mathematical community to make mathematics accessible to all students; all students have the right to learn "real" math—not just arithmetic and computation. Perhaps the most powerful messages of the standards were the goals, which stated that in a technological society, students should see mathematics as a powerful problem-solving tool, be confident in their ability to do math, and learn to communicate and reason mathematically. In addition, the NCTM standards are mathematical strands that are to be interwoven and connected into meaningful lessons. This format allows us to integrate and connect mathematics to the lives of our students.

MULTIPLE INTELLIGENCES AND THE MATHEMATICS CLASSROOM

The NCTM standards make reference to what and how students learn. What do we know about cognition and learning styles? In Howard Gardner's *Frames of Mind,* intelligence is defined as being more than "short answers to short questions—answers that predict academic success" (Gardner 1985, 4). Gardner states that "a human intellectual competence must entail a set of skills of problem solving—enabling the individual to resolve genuine problems or difficulties that he or she encounters and, when appropriate, to create an effective product—and must also entail the potential for *finding or creating problems*—thereby laying the groundwork for the acquisition of new knowledge" (Gardner 1985, 60–61).

Drawing from the framework of cognitive and developmental psychology, Gardner presents a case for the existence of multiple intelligences, which if used in an educational setting can enhance a student's opportunities and options. If we wish to expand the mathematical horizons of our students, we must examine Gardner's theories and see how they can be incorporated into the teaching and learning of mathematics. Let's look at each intelligence as described by Howard Gardner.

Verbal/Linguistic Intelligence

The verbal/linguistic intelligence is concerned with the use of language. People who possess this intelligence to a heightened degree have a strong sensitivity to the meaning of words, are able to communicate effectively, and are generally comfortable using language in verbal and written forms. We can encourage this type of intelligence in the mathematics classroom by (1) encouraging students working in groups to communicate their mathematical ideas, and (2) requiring students to express their answers in linguistic and symbolic forms.

Musical/Rhythmic Intelligence

Each of us has musical capabilities to some degree. People with a highly developed musical/rhythmic intelligence enjoy and understand music and may become singers, composers, or conductors. While we can't directly encourage the development of this intelligence in the math classroom, we can present activities that are congruent with the interests of these students; for example, there are close connections between rhythms and fractions. Some activities addressing these connections are included in this book.

Logical/Mathematical Intelligence

People who have a strong propensity for mathematics are typically characterized by a love for the problem-solving process, using patterns, reasoning, and symbolic abstractions. Mathematics can be divided into two branches: applied and theoretical. It is the field of theoretical mathematics that builds theories and tests them with abstract logic, but it is the field of applied mathematics that encourages us to solve problems in the "real world." Both are essential contributors to our body of mathematical knowledge, but it is the applied mathematics that brings mathematics to life in the classroom. We can encourage our students to develop this intelligence by giving them the opportunity to participate in activities and projects that are meaningful and demonstrate the power and usefulness of mathematics.

Visual/Spatial Intelligence

People with a strongly developed visual/spatial intelligence have the ability to accurately and effortlessly understand their physical world. Research has indicated that students who have a more strongly developed spatial intelligence find math less threatening and are better math students. Growth in this area can be encouraged through activities and projects.

Bodily/Kinesthetic Intelligence

People with a strong bodily/kinesthetic intelligence have the ability to "use one's body in highly differentiated and skilled ways . . . to work skillfully with objects, both those that involve the fine motor movements of one's fingers and hands and those that exploit gross motor movements of the body" (Gardner 1985, 206). Permitting students to work with manipulatives and encouraging the concrete, physical representation of mathematics concepts improves bodily/kinesthetic intelligence and brings comfort to students who excel in this area.

Intrapersonal Intelligence

Understanding and awareness of one's own feelings and thoughts are at the center of this intelligence. By encouraging students to explain their reasoning and thinking, they become more self-reflective. Not only does the traditional review-teach-practice paradigm inhibit the growth of mathematical reasoning, it discourages the development of intrapersonal intelligence.

Interpersonal Intelligence

Sensitivity toward others and the world around them is the trademark of those who possess interpersonal intelligence to a high degree. The traditional mathematics classroom is usually more competitive than collaborative in nature. The activities and projects presented in this book are designed to foster collaboration and encourage students to work together toward a common goal. These lessons cultivate the growth of interpersonal intelligence as they develop deeper math concepts.

Naturalist Intelligence

Recently, Gardner has suggested the addition of an eighth intelligence—the intelligence of the *naturalist* (Gardner 1995). He describes individuals who possess this eighth intelligence as people who can make distinctions between and classify flora and fauna. Children who can "make acute discriminations among cars, sneakers, or hairstyles" (Gardner 1995, 206) exemplify naturalists in our modern society.

While students may strongly perceive themselves as having a particular mode of thought, each possesses all eight intelligences. These can be developed to some reasonable level if educators focus on more than mathematical and verbal intelligence. In addition, if we, as teachers, recognize the different intelligences of our students, we give them an opportunity to shine and be recognized for their particular talents.

MANIPULATIVES, ACTIVITIES, AND PROJECTS

Not only are manipulatives, activities, and projects powerful tools to teach mathematics, they also allow us to augment our teaching styles, thereby respecting the multiple intelligences and modes of thought of our students. The chart on the next page describes the attributes of each of these classroom strategies (some of the attributes overlap).

Attributes	Manipulative	Activity	Project
Draws upon a student's capacity for visual thinking and encourages visual/spatial intelligence.	Yes	No	No
Helps students develop an understanding of concepts using concrete models.	Yes	No	No
Helps students remember concepts by giving them a visual model.	Yes	Yes	Yes
Usually allows for a variety of problem-solving strategies, encouraging students to use an intelligence that is congruent with their learning style.	Yes	Yes	Yes
Can be designed so students can work in collaborative groups, encouraging students to develop their interpersonal intelligence.	Yes	Yes	Yes
Allows students to draw upon previous experiences and construct knowledge.	No	Yes	Yes
Reflects "real-life" problems and encourages students to see powerful applications.	No	Yes	Yes
Can be integrated into standard curriculum as enrichment.	Yes	Yes	Yes
Can be solved using a variety of methods and styles.	Yes	Yes	Yes
Allows students to investigate problems over an extended period of time.	No	Yes	Yes
Can be designed to draw upon a student's interests and abilities.	Yes	Yes	Yes
Brings a variety of skills and concepts into an on-going activity.	Yes	Yes	Yes

The activities and projects contained in this book are designed to be congruent with three underlying philosophies:

1. The curricular foundation—the NCTM's *Curriculum and Evaluation Standards for School Mathematics*. Each of the lessons incorporates problem solving, reasoning, connections, and communication into its framework.

2. The psychological foundation—Howard Gardner's *Frames of Mind.* Students should be more comfortable and encouraged to "grow" mathematically with lessons that provide brain-compatible structures.

3. The pedagogical foundation—manipulatives, activities, and projects, which invite the active, rather than passive, involvement of students. In such a classroom environment, students are enthusiastically involved in the learning process; they are communicating and reasoning mathematically. The classroom is exciting and electric with learning!

MATHEMATICS AND THE "REAL WORLD"

How often have we heard in the math classroom, "When are we ever going to use this?" This question is asked because, all too often, skills are isolated from their applications in the "real world." We teach students how to multiply and use story problems to apply the mutiplication skills. Is this the only way to learn how to multiply?

The philosophy behind the activities and projects in this book is that (1) students will learn a skill when they need to use it, and (2) students need to use a skill over a period of time to learn it. With this in mind, students are actively involved in real-world problems. Connections made between mathematics and other curriculum areas are repeated throughout the book and are intertwined through appropriate activities.

The NCTM's standards characterize mathematics as problem solving, communication, reasoning, and connections. The activities and projects in *Multiple Intelligences in the Mathematics Classroom* have been designed to focus on each of these and encourage their integration into the classroom. Mathematics can be a means for students to explain and explore the world around them; the foundation is problem solving:

> Classrooms with a problem-solving orientation are permeated by thought-provoking questions, speculations, investigations, and explorations. . . . (NCTM 1989, 23)

It has been said that if children cannot explain how they got their answers, they really didn't understand how to solve the problems. Students need to have "many opportunities to communicate their mathematical ideas. . . . Opportunities to explain, conjecture, and defend one's ideas orally and in writing can stimulate deeper understandings of concepts and principles" (NCTM 1989, 78). Most of the activities in this book require students, working with others, to explain their reasoning and how they obtained their solutions. This type of mathematical communication requires reflection and accomplishes two things: (1) it helps students better understand symbolic mathematics, and (2) it permits students to share the varied methodologies used by other groups.

For students to believe that they can do mathematics, they need to justify their thinking and develop confidence in their reasoning abilities. For many students, math is not a sense-making experience. They are given a rule and told to practice it, memorize it, and learn it. If they forget the rule, then what? "A climate should be established in the classroom that places critical thinking at the heart of instruction. . . . Children need to know that being able to explain and justify their thinking is important and that how a problem is solved is as important as its answer" (NCTM 1989, 29). This type of classroom climate is the heart of the "mathematics as reasoning" standard.

The mathematics curriculum is usually described by the scope and sequence of isolated topics. If we taught reading with the same strategies we use to teach math, students would be required to memorize all the words of a story before reading it! Mathematical applications have great significance to students, and by making connections to these real-world applications, students realize the importance and power of mathematics. The "mathematics as connection" standard encourages making connections in two ways: (1) between the various strands of mathematics, and (2) between mathematics and other disciplines. The activities in this book attempt to accomplish both of these goals. Because the skills and concepts have not been isolated into artificial and arbitrary segments, students have the opportunity to practice the skills and develop the concepts necessary to solve a *real problem*.

ALTERNATIVE ASSESSMENT

If we change what we teach in mathematics and the way we teach it, can we maintain traditional methods of assessment?

The NCTM assessment standards state that "all aspects of school mathematics—content, teaching, and assessment—need to change on a systemic basis" (NCTM 1995, 2). The Mathematical Sciences Education Board suggests that "assessment should reflect the mathematics that is most important for students to learn" (NCTM 1993, 32).

Traditionally, assessment of students' learning in math has had a narrow focus and vision. The focus has been on paper-and-pencil tests; the vision has been to give the students a grade. The most common strategies are quizzes and tests. Paper-and-pencil tests are extremely limited for these reasons: (1) they measure only specific, easily tested skills and recollection of specific facts, (2) they are rarely used to influence the instructional process, and (3) they may not even be a valid indication of what the student knows because of the test's limited scope.

Because of changes in mathematics instruction, some important issues of assessment face the educational community. Here is a listing of some of the concerns:

- Standardized tests do not evaluate an activity-based, problem-solving curriculum.

- Closed or forced-response tests do not, themselves, give us an adequate picture of a student's capabilities.

- Assessment of students should allow for their unique modes of learning and should enable them to present their knowledge in their own style.

- Assessment should provide opportunities for learning; it should be a beginning, not an end.

- Mathematics curriculum and assessment should be integrated with other subject areas.

- Many educators feel that the traditional standardized achievement test may be a factor in lowering achievement in mathematics because it tests computation in isolation.

The new evaluation standards (NCTM 1995) ask schools to shift to a system based on multiple sources that rely on the professional judgment of teachers. The assessment techniques suggested with the activities and projects in this book are performance based and adhere to the recommendations of those advocating reform in mathematics. In addition, it is suggested that portfolios be used to keep the students' work and to assess their progress and mathematical growth.

The Grading Matrix

The grading matrix serves an important role for both teacher and students. As a teacher, it allows you to determine what mathematical concepts and ideas are important to the lesson, how the lesson fits into your instruction and curriculum, and what mathematical and nonmathematical activities you value in the lesson. The grading matrix is a valuable tool for students as well. It communicates to them what it is you value in the lesson and how their understanding will be evaluated. Sample matrices have been supplied with each lesson as a guide for instruction. As you change the lessons and adapt them to your classroom, consideration should be given to changing the matrix to align it with your instruction.

Observation

Observation of students affords the teacher the opportunity to assess understanding, performance in a small group, problem-solving approaches, thinking processes, understanding

Observation Sheet		
Student	**Class**	
Date	**Activity**	**Observation**

Student Observation Checklist				
Name of Student				
Date				
Criteria	**4**	**3**	**2**	**1**
Student demonstrates that he/she understands the lesson (concepts)				
Problem-solving strategies and processes are being used to solve the problem				
Student is actively participating in the working of the group				
Student is communicating his/her ideas to the group in a constructive manner				
Overall assessment during today's observation				

of concepts, and communication skills. In a normal classroom, it is not possible to observe each student every day, but it is possible to rotate observations so that each student is observed at least once each grading period. Two different sample observation forms are included above.

Portfolios

Portfolios are representative samples of students' work collected over a period of time. A portfolios tells the story of a student's growth and mathematical development; it is not just a folder to keep work in. It should contain illustrative samples, such as

- solutions to nonroutine problems

- examples of problem-solving activities

- journal entries

- teacher checklists and matrices

- examples of projects

- pictures that students have used to define a concept

- an applied use of mathematics (may include work done across disciplines)

- a student's explanation for each entry

- selected homework

- other items that can be used to examine student progress and growth

Originally, all of a student's work can be placed into a work portfolio; then, it can be selectively transferred to an assessment portfolio, which becomes representative of the student's work. Below is a sample form that can be used for students to explain their placement of each entry.

Portfolio Selection

Name _____

Date _____

This work is an example of:

☐   My problem-solving skills

☐   My reasoning and critical-thinking skills

☐   My communication skills

☐   How math connects to other subjects

Why _____

_____

_____

_____

_____

_____

Other Assessments

If problem solving, communication, and reasoning are to be the focus of school mathematics, they should be the focus of assessment. Each of these abilities develops over an extended period of time, and each child has his or her unique rate of growth. How can we assess these aspects of a mathematics program? A student's ability to solve problems can be assessed through observations, discussion, homework, journal writing, or successful completion of mathematical tasks that focus on problem solving.

Mathematical communication can be assessed by examining both the verbal and written fluency of students. Listen to their discussions within their groups, how well they follow oral directions, and the quality of their journal entries.

Students should be encouraged to share their reasoning with the class, and their ideas and strategies should be accepted nonjudgmentally. Very often, students are afraid to share their thinking because they are shy and fearful that if they are wrong, they will be embarrassed. Classrooms should be "thought-protected zones"—all thoughts and conjectures should be welcomed and applauded. It serves no purpose to say to a child, "No, that's wrong!" Try saying, "That's very interesting. Does anyone have another idea?" or "Did anyone solve it a different way?" How powerful for a child to discover his or her own error and then say, "I'd like to change my answer—I think Mary was right because. . . . "

Assessment that is designed to be congruent with a particular mathematical task uses strategies appropriate for the activity, helps foster persistence, encourages thinking in a variety of styles, and allows for multiple avenues to approach a problem (thus making it accessible to more students.)

HOW TO USE THIS BOOK

Each of the activities in this book consists of three major sections: the teacher's page, the activity pages (blacklines), and the grading matrix. Following is a description of the teacher's page and the grading matrix.

The Teacher's Page

The format of the teacher's page is meant to define curriculum areas and intelligences, outline concepts and skills, set procedures and activities, allow for lesson variation, and tie assessment to the instruction in multiple ways. Each contains the following sections: "Math Topics," "Types of Intelligences," "Concepts," "Materials," "What to Do," "Variation," and "Assessment." They are designed to explain the activities and make it easier to use them in your classroom.

Math Topics

"Math Topics" is a description of the mathematics presented in the activity. In all cases, more than one topic is addressed, since, in the real world, math topics are never isolated into neat and separate strands. It is not expected or presumed that you will have taught any or all of the mathematics topics prior to using the activity. As in most other curricula areas, students can learn the necessary math skills as they work through the problem. Your students will be learning mathematics through their problem-solving efforts.

Types of Intelligences

"Types of Intelligences" includes the areas of intelligences, as defined by Gardner, that students might use when working through the activity. Because many of the problems are open ended and can be solved in multiple ways, students have the opportunity to explore and experiment with different strategies and solutions. Students are accustomed to learning math by manipulating symbols and memorizing rules. For those whose logical/mathematical intelligence is strong and well developed, this method is usually successful. Unfortunately, only about 25 percent of students have real strengths in this type of intelligence. The activities in *Multiple Intelligences in the Mathematics Classroom* allow students to develop problem-solving strategies that are congruent with their intellectual strengths. By allowing our students to draw pictures (visual/spatial), write in their journals (verbal/linguistic), work within cooperative groups (interpersonal) or, perhaps, measure and pace off distances (bodily/kinesthetic), we are respecting their multiple intelligences and increasing the possibility of their success.

Concepts

"Concepts" delineates the skills students will use while solving the problem. Assessment criteria are gleaned from this section. If one of the concepts is to estimate the length of a dollar bill, it is reasonable to evaluate a student's proficiency at estimating length. A careful examination of "Concepts" will explain the skills, facts, and strategies students will use and will allow you, as the teacher, to tie your assessment into your instruction.

Materials

The "Materials" section lists the supplies and materials needed for students to begin the activity. For example, if an overhead transparency is needed for follow-up work with students, it will be listed in this section. If calculators are listed, they are necessary because of the complexity of the computations. Having these supplies and materials on hand will help make the activity run smoothly and efficiently.

What to Do

How do you set up the lesson? Read the "What to Do" section. While this section is not meant to be a step-by-step outline, it does give the teacher an idea of how to begin and of what might happen. Most often, this section begins with a question to be posed to the students. For example, "What do you think will happen if . . . ?" "Have you ever considered the possibility that . . . ?" or "How do you think we might attempt to figure that out?" You would *never* want to say something like, "Don't do it that way" or "You must always do it this way." Instead, serve as a facilitator or guide to the students. I would caution you to follow two very important rules:

1. Go with the flow—give your students the opportunity to explore their own solutions. It is amazing the creativity students will use when they can plan and organize in a cooperative group.

2. Don't be the sage on the stage—don't feel that you must tell your students "how to do it" or what the answer is. Give them the opportunity to experiment with various strategies and use their multiple intelligences. When you give students a "rule" you are limiting their solution strategies to one right way.

Variation

This section describes an extension for the activity. It might extend the activity to a longer project; it might develop the same concepts using additional activities; or it might be something that challenges your "better" math students. Use your creativity—add variations and design your own activities using the materials and models supplied in this book.

Assessment

To give you a more complete picture of each student, the "Assessment" section looks at a variety of criteria:

- *Student products* are authentic—what did the students produce?

- *Student observation* provides us with a view of the students' actions and allows us to question and discuss ideas with them during their work.

- The *grading matrix* reflects the concepts and skills of the lesson. It ties instruction to assessment.

- The *journal question(s)* provides students an opportunity to express their knowledge using language rather than mathematical symbols and rules. Expressing their thoughts in this way encourages students to make connections between the application of mathematics (expressed through the activity) and the skill or concept (the mathematics curriculum). A pictorial explanation of these connections might look like the illustration below.

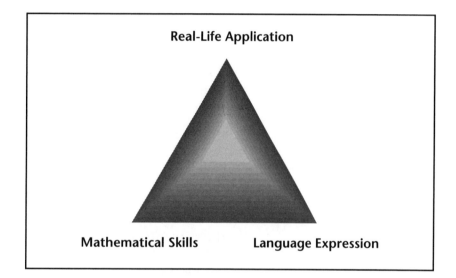

Real-Life Application

Mathematical Skills   **Language Expression**

The Grading Matrix

To improve the total quality of math instruction, we need to examine what is taught (the curriculum), how it is taught (the pedagogy), and how we evaluate what our students have learned (assessment). The activities presented in this book require the students to perform tasks that are open ended rather than tightly structured. These types of tasks require students to problem-solve solution strategies. The tasks may not have a clear path to an answer and may lead to other problems. These types of performance tasks require the use of assessment techniques and evaluation methods that differ from the more traditional methods. Some aspects of assessment and evaluation have been discussed earlier, but at this time I would like to look at the grading matrix and one aspect of the evaluation process.

The NCTM's *Assessment Standards for School Mathematics* (1995) defines evaluation as "the process of determining the worth of, or assigning a value to, something on the basis of careful examination and judgment" (p. 3). The grading matrix is an evaluation instrument that allows for the examination and valuing of different aspects of the activity. The matrix contains two dimensions: a 4-3-2-1 scale that allows the teacher to rate the quality of work on a range from excellent to poor, and the set of criteria being rated. These criteria vary with the activity and the concepts and skills to be learned. By tying the criteria to a particular lesson, we have the opportunity to make a strong connection between instruction and assessment.

Let's examine the 4-3-2-1 scale first. What characteristics would determine each of these ratings? In the simplest sense, a 4 would equate with excellent work, a 3 with average work, a 2 with below average work, and a 1 with poor work. Since these ratings are used for a variety of activities (computations, problem-solving tasks, written responses, and collaborative skills), it is necessary to define the rating within each context.

The criteria are gleaned from the concepts and skills required of the activity. If an activity requires measurement, how well did the students measure? If the activity requires estimation, how well did the students estimate? How well did the students work together? Student products are used to assess some of the criteria, while observation and written journals are used for others.

This type of assessment is authentic, meaningful, and gives a more accurate picture of the progress students are making in the classroom than a paper-and-pencil test. It is possible that some of the activities could be concluded with traditional evaluation; however, these are not supplied with the activities.

An overview, in table form, of the activities and mathematics topics they address can be found after the table of contents. I hope the activities in this book not only enrich your mathematics curriculum but help your students see the relevance and power of math in their everyday lives. Sit back and enjoy your math lessons—your students will!

Estimation, Large Numbers, and Numeration

CHAPTER 1

Estimation, Large Numbers, and Numeration

Mathematics can be a powerful tool for students to make sense of the world around them. Without good estimation skills, we cannot approximate distances, or the number of people in a crowd, or how much our grocery bill will be by looking at a shopping cart full of groceries. Without an adequate understanding of large numbers, we cannot conceive of the enormity of a deficit of $5,000,000,000,000 (five trillion dollars) or the need to change an area code to provide the telephone company with additional telephone numbers. But, all too often, classroom math is seen as a set of rules and exercises, a collection of isolated facts that have little relationship to the real world of students. The activities in this chapter will encourage students to do the following:

- Estimate when working with large numbers and distances in real-life problems

- Problem-solve strategies to find reasonable answers

- Experience the visual patterns formed by number patterns

- Use manipulatives to make connections between abstract concepts and the concrete models that represent them

The first two activities in this chapter are designed to give students experiences that relate large numbers to physical models in the real world; the last three activities connect number theory and number patterns with geometric models, color patterns, and Venn diagrams. By working together, students are given the opportunity to develop their intrapersonal and interpersonal intelligences and, depending on the group's strategies, heighten their visual/spatial, bodily/kinesthetic, logical/mathematical, and/or verbal/ linguistic intelligences.

$1,000,000 LONG

This first activity is an open-ended problem that encourages students to explore strategies, work collaboratively, make mathematical connections to social studies, and examine alternative solutions when dealing with large numbers. This activity addresses questions such as, "If your group placed a million dollars end to end, how far would they reach?" "Would they reach across a football field? Across your state? Across the United States? Across the world?" A dollar bill is *approximately* 6.25 inches long, but not exactly! How precise must our measurements be? Can they be exact? This activity is perfect for an authentic discussion of "how precise is precise?"

HOW MANY STRIDES TO WALK AROUND THE EARTH?

The second activity is another open-ended problem that requires each group to develop its own unique problem-solving strategies when pacing off a very large number of steps. The initial problem necessitates figuring out what a normal stride is. In the process of solving this problem, students work collaboratively, make mathematical connections to science, and use rounded numbers as they ponder precision and accuracy.

PATTERNS IN THE 100S CHART

The third activity moves from estimation and large numbers to numeracy and mathematical patterns. Seeing patterns in mathematics is an important step in developing mathematical reasoning. "Creating and extending patterns . . . and recognizing relationships within patterns require children to apply analytical and spatial reasoning" (NCTM 1989, 30). Students are asked to be mathematically creative and design a pattern on the 100s chart from a sequence of numbers. This activity fills the bill for those who have a highly developed visual/spatial intelligence and prefer visual models to abstract numerical patterns. In addition, by verbally describing the pattern, students are communicating mathematically and developing their verbal/linguistic intelligence.

RECTANGLES AND FACTORS

In the fourth activity, students use square tiles to discover the relationship between rectangular arrays and prime and composite numbers. How many rectangles can be formed that have an area of 7? An area of 12? When students use manipulative materials and reasoning skills to discover an abstract relationship, the learning is more meaningful and permanent. Like Activity 3, this activity meets the needs of students with a high degree of visual/spatial intelligence. By associating numbers with their factors in an area model, these students acquire a deeper and longer-lasting understanding.

VENN DIAGRAMS: LCM AND GCF

The final activity develops mathematical reasoning with the help of Venn diagrams and prime factors. The visual model supplied by the Venn diagram helps students understand the intersection and union of the prime factors of a pair of numbers in a unique graphic mode. Combining a mathematical concept from abstract number theory with its visual representation brings it into the "mind's eye" of the student.

The NCTM standards state, "If children are to develop good number concepts, considerable instructional time must be devoted to number and numeration" (1989, 38). What better way to develop good number concepts than through interesting and motivating activities that are congruent with the multiple intelligences of your students!

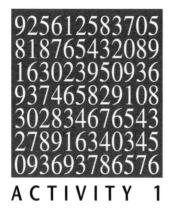

$1,000,000 Long

MATH TOPICS

numeration, estimation, computation with large numbers, problem solving, mathematical connections

---

TYPES OF INTELLIGENCES

logical/mathematical, visual/spatial, bodily/kinesthetic, interpersonal, intrapersonal, verbal/linguistic

---

CONCEPTS

Students will do the following:

1. Estimate the length of one million dollar bills

2. Work collaboratively to develop problem-solving strategies

3. Measure one bill and compute the length of one million bills

4. Convert their results to appropriate units of measure

5. Use a map to determine the distance

6. Discover important landmarks within a circle of a determined radius

MATERIALS

rulers, dollar bills, maps, calculators, "$1,000,000 Long" worksheets

WHAT TO DO

Hold up a dollar bill and ask, "How long do you think this is?" Then ask, "If we placed one million of these end to end, how far do you think they would reach?"

Give students a copy of the blackline master "$1,000,000 Long" and have them estimate, in groups, how far the bills would reach. Materials should be available for the groups to use to solve the problem. Have each group record their estimate on their worksheet in the space provided.

For teacher use only: A dollar bill is approximately 6.25 inches long; one million would be approximately 6,250,000 inches, or 520,833.3 feet, or 98.6 miles long.

To encourage mathematical reasoning, it is important for students to write a detailed explanation of where they could travel and how they calculated the distance.

VARIATION

Have students find the area of a circle formed with a 98.6-mile radius and find all important landmarks within that area.

ASSESSMENT

1. Observation of student groups

2. Grading matrix

3. Journal question: "How far do you think $1 billion would reach? Explain your reasoning."

$1,000,000 Long
Worksheet

Names _____

_____

Date _____ Class _____

If your group placed one million one-dollar bills end to end, how far would they reach? Do you think they would reach across a football field? Across your state? Across the United States? Across the world? Write your estimate here:

_____

Working with your group, use a dollar bill, a ruler, and a calculator to determine how far one million bills would actually reach. Be sure to express your distance using reasonable units of measure. Write an explanation of your reasoning and calculations below. Use a map to determine how far you could travel. Where could you go? How did you figure that out?

_____

_____

_____

_____

How does this answer compare with your initial estimate? How would you rate your estimate?

_____

_____

_____

What other cities or landmarks fall within the calculated distance?

_____

_____

_____

$1,000,000 Long
Grading Matrix

Names _____

_____

_____

_____

Date _____   Class _____

Criteria	4	3	2	1
Accuracy of measurement				
Accuracy of computations				
Quality of problem-solving strategies				
Map work accurate and distance computed correctly				
How well group worked together				

Comments:

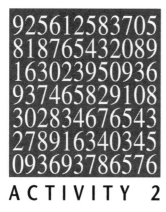

How Many Strides to Walk around the Earth?

MATH TOPICS

numeration, estimation, computation with large numbers, measurement, problem solving with large numbers, averages, mathematical connections, reasoning

---

TYPES OF INTELLIGENCES

logical/mathematical, visual/spatial, bodily/kinesthetic, intrapersonal, interpersonal, verbal/linguistic

---

CONCEPTS

Students will do the following:

1. Work collaboratively to problem solve the length of a normal stride

2. Accurately measure the length of their strides

3. Find the average length of a stride for their group

4. Compute the number of "normal" strides it would take to walk around the earth

---

MATERIALS

meter- or yardsticks (or tapes); copies of "How Many Strides to Walk around the Earth?" worksheet 1; calculators; over-

---

head transparency of "How Many Strides to Walk around the Earth?" worksheet 2

WHAT TO DO

Begin activity by asking, "How many strides do you think you would take if you were to walk around the earth's equator?" It is important for students to understand that it takes two steps to form one stride. Demonstrate a two-step stride. Ask students if they believe this is a normal stride. Students should see that one stride cannot be considered "normal"; we need to take multiple strides (twenty or more) and divide the total distance by the number of strides to find the average length of just one.

Place students in collaborative groups of four, give them the materials they need, and have them proceed to solve the problem. When group averages have been calculated, bring the class back together to find the length of an average stride for the class. Analyze the results for variance.

VARIATION

Have students compute the number of strides to walk to the moon (an average distance of 384,000 km, or 239,000 mi.).

ASSESSMENT

1. Observation of student groups

2. Grading matrix

3. Journal questions:

   a. "Why did your group use the mean length of your strides to solve the problem?"

   b. "It would take a train traveling 100 kph (161 mph) about 99.5 days to reach the moon. How long would you estimate it would take (on the average) for you to walk there?"

How Many Strides to Walk around the Earth?
Worksheet 1

Suppose you went on a long hike around the earth's equator. How many strides would it take?

Names _____

Date _____   Class _____

Directions: A stride is the distance you travel after walking two steps. For example, if you start walking with your left foot, when your right foot touches the ground, you have walked one stride. In groups, problem-solve how you might find a normal stride for each member; then measure the length of a stride for each member of your group and enter these measurements on the table below. Find the mean (or average) length of one stride for the members of your group. But first, in the space provided below, describe what you will do to determine a "normal" stride.

_____

_____

_____

Name of Person	Length of Stride
Mean Length of Stride	

The distance around the earth at the equator is about 40,000,000 meters, or about 24,000 miles. About how many strides would it take to walk around the world? Use the stride length computed from your group's experiment. _____

_____

How Many Strides to Walk around the Earth?
Worksheet 2

Class Data Sheet

Group	Mean Length of Stride

Mean Length of Stride for Class:	

Is there a difference between the mean for the length of a stride for individual groups and the whole class? If there is, why do you think this occurred?

How Many Strides to Walk around the Earth?
Grading Matrix

Names _____

_____

_____

_____

Date _____   Class _____

Criteria	4	3	2	1
Accuracy of measurements				
Accuracy of computations				
Criteria group used to determine the length of one stride				
How well group worked together				
Completeness of data collection sheet				
Comments:				

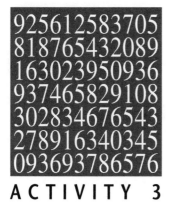

ACTIVITY 3

Patterns in the 100s Chart

MATH TOPICS

numeration, number patterns, reasoning, mathematical communication

---

TYPES OF INTELLIGENCES

logical/mathematical, visual/spatial, verbal/linguistic, naturalist

---

CONCEPTS

Students will do the following:

1. Think of a number pattern

2. Create a visual representation of that pattern on the 100s chart

3. Describe, in writing, what their number pattern looks like

---

MATERIALS

"Patterns in the 100s Chart" worksheets; markers, colored pencils, or crayons

WHAT TO DO

Discuss with students the possible number patterns they might use. They can color in the multiples of numbers, even or odd numbers, numbers whose sum is 9, etc. Discuss which patterns might have more members than others and which might make more attractive designs.

Give students time, in groups or pairs, to create their designs, then bring the class back together and allow students to present their creations and discuss their patterns. (This is important to encourage mathematical communication.)

VARIATION

Students can be introduced to more difficult number theory concepts (e.g., the set of primes, multiples of the first perfect number, etc.).

ASSESSMENT

1. Grading matrix

2. Journal question: "Describe the design that your number pattern made on the chart. How do you think it could have been improved?"

Patterns in the 100s Chart
Worksheet

Names _____

Date _____   Class _____

Think of a number pattern. It can be multiples of 3, even numbers, numbers whose digits add up to 6, etc. Be creative. Discuss various possibilities with your partner or other group member. Each of you may choose a different pattern and try it out. Here is my number pattern:

1	2	3	4	5	6	7	8	9	10
11	12	13	14	15	16	17	18	19	20
21	22	23	24	25	26	27	28	29	30
31	32	33	34	35	36	37	38	39	40
41	42	43	44	45	46	47	48	49	50
51	52	53	54	55	56	57	58	59	60
61	62	63	64	65	66	67	68	69	70
71	72	73	74	75	76	77	78	79	80
81	82	83	84	85	86	87	88	89	90
91	92	93	94	95	96	97	98	99	100

Describe what your pattern looks like: _____

_____

_____

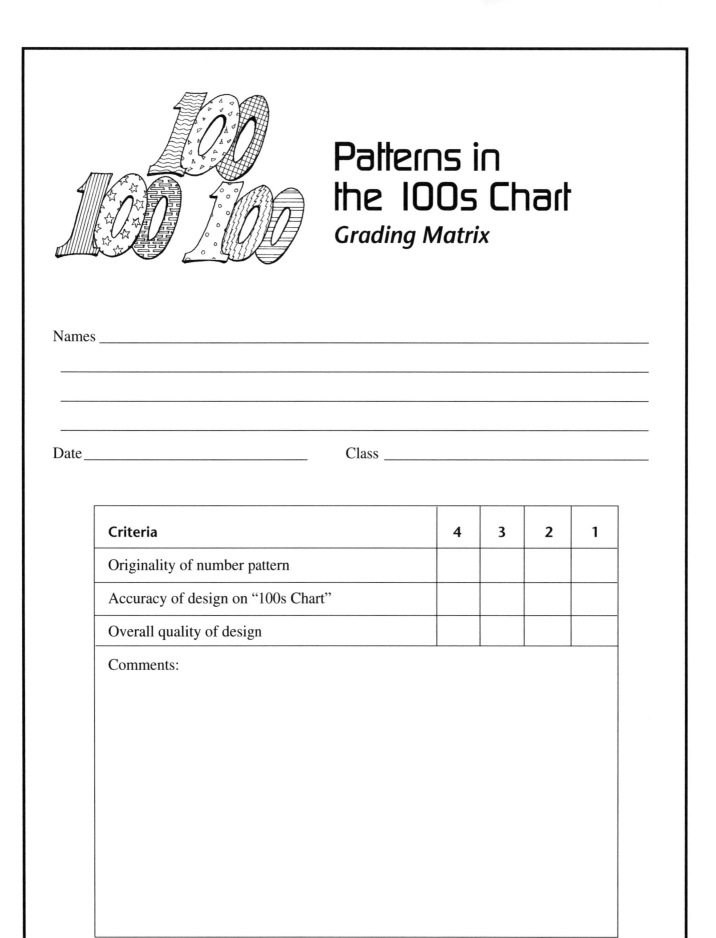

Patterns in the 100s Chart
Grading Matrix

Names _____

_____

_____

_____

Date _____   Class _____

Criteria	4	3	2	1
Originality of number pattern				
Accuracy of design on "100s Chart"				
Overall quality of design				
Comments:				

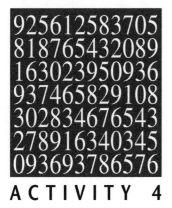

ACTIVITY 4

Rectangles and Factors

MATH TOPICS

numeration, factors, area, prime and composite numbers

TYPES OF INTELLIGENCES

logical/mathematical, visual/spatial, verbal/linguistic, interpersonal

---

CONCEPTS

Students will do the following:

1. Use manipulatives to form rectangles

2. Understand that the sides of these rectangles are factors of the area

3. Discover the difference between prime and composite numbers

---

MATERIALS

buckets of square tiles (cardboard tiles can be used); "Rectangles and Factors" worksheets; overhead tiles for demonstration

WHAT TO DO

Place twelve overhead tiles on the overhead projector and ask for student volunteers to place these tiles into rectangular arrays. Some possibilities are 1 x 12, 2 x 6, and 3 x 4. (For the purposes of this activity, a 1 x 12 and a 12 x 1 will be considered the same array.) The possibilities will look like this:

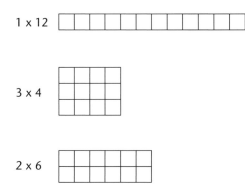

1 x 12

3 x 4

2 x 6

Students will discover that prime numbers have only one rectangular array, whereas composite numbers have at least two. Place students into pairs, with the necessary manipulatives, and give them time to find the factors of each of the twenty numbers.

VARIATION

Students can be encouraged to find the prime factors of each of the numbers and, using combinations, find the integral factors. For example: the prime factors of 12 are 2 x 2 x 3; the combinations are 2^0, 2^1, 2^2, 3^1, 2^1 x 3^1, and 2^2 x 3^1. This activity gives them the opportunity to work with concrete materials and abstract concepts simultaneously.

ASSESSMENT

1. Observation of student pairs

2. Grading matrix

3. Journal question: "Explain the relationship between the number of rectangles and whether the number is prime or composite."

Rectangles and Factors
Worksheet

Names _____

Date _____   Class _____

Directions: Use your tiles to form all the rectangles that contain the number of tiles called for. You may sketch or describe each of the rectangles in the space provided. Then record the factors for each rectangle.

Number of Tiles	Description of Rectangles (l x w)	List of factors
1		
2		
3		
4		
5		
6		
7		
8		
9		
10		
11		
12		
13		
14		

Write your observations about the size of the rectangles and their factors here:

_____

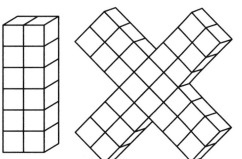 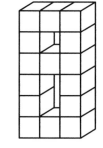

Rectangles and Factors
Grading Matrix

Names _____

_____

_____

_____

Date _____   Class _____

Criteria	4	3	2	1
All possibilities are recorded				
Data is correct				
How well pair worked together				

Comments:

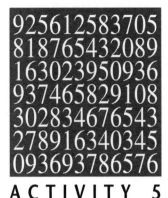

Venn Diagrams: LCM and GCF

MATH TOPICS

numeration, number theory, reasoning, Venn diagrams

TYPES OF INTELLIGENCES

logical/mathematical, visual/spatial, interpersonal

CONCEPTS

Students will do the following:

1. Find the prime factors of a pair of numbers

2. Place the factors correctly in a Venn diagram

3. Understand the relationship between the intersection of the sets and the GCF (greatest common factor)

4. Understand the relationship between the union of the sets and the LCM (least common multiple)

MATERIALS

"Venn Diagrams: LCM and GCF" worksheets

WHAT TO DO

Place students into pairs and discuss the Venn diagram and the purpose of each of the sections. A good example:

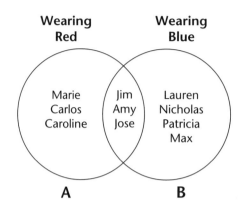

This simple diagram helps explain the reasoning behind the placement within the diagram.

Additional questions: (1) Who are all the students in this group? (This is the union of the two sets: A∪B.); (2) Who are the students wearing both red and blue? (This is the intersection of the two sets: A∩B.)

Students can now work in pairs, following these steps: (1) choose two numbers, (2) find the prime factors of each number, (3) place the numbers correctly in the Venn diagram, and (4) find the union (LCM) and intersection (GCF) of the two numbers.

VARIATION

Expand the activity to include Venn diagrams that examine subset relationships (4 and 8) and the LCM and GCF of three numbers.

ASSESSMENT

1. Observation of student pairs

2. Grading matrix

3. Journal question: "Describe the differences between these Venn diagrams: (6 and 8) and (8 and 24)."

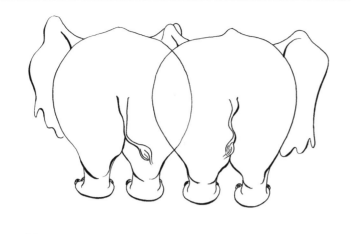

Venn Diagrams: LCM and GCF

Worksheet

Names _____

_____

Date _____   Class _____

Directions:

1. Find the prime factors of your numbers.
2. When the two numbers share a factor, place that factor in the intersection of the two circles.

Remember: The intersection of the two circles is the GCF (greatest common factor). The union of the two circles is the LCM (least common multiple).

> Example: Let's look at 12 and 16
> The prime factors of 12 are 2 x 2 x 3
> The prime factors of 16 are 2 x 2 x 2 x 2
> The intersection, 4, is the GCF
> The union, 48, is the LCM

My two numbers are: _____

Their prime factors are: _____

_____

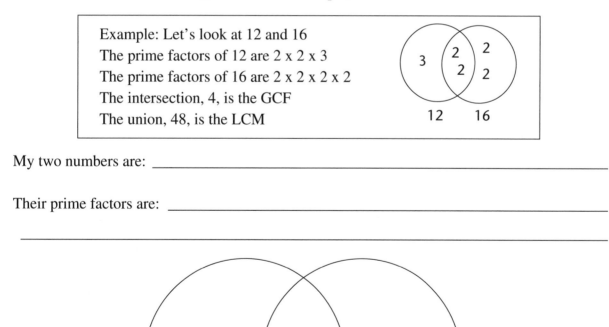

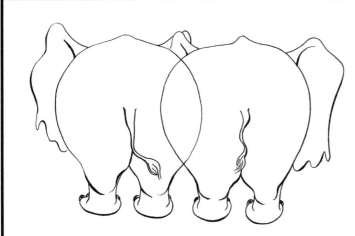

Venn Diagrams: LCM and GCF
Grading Matrix

Names _____

_____

_____

_____

Date _____   Class _____

Criteria	4	3	2	1
Accuracy of prime factors				
Placement of prime factors				
How well pair worked together				
Comments:				

CHAPTER 2

Applying Fractions and Decimals in the "Real World"

CHAPTER 2

Applying Fractions and Decimals in the "Real World"

We spend a great deal of instructional time helping students master isolated facts and rules and little time exploring how they relate to one another and to applications in the "real world." "As students expand their mathematical horizons to include fractions, decimals, integers, and rational numbers . . . they need to understand both the common ideas underlying these number systems and the differences among them" (NCTM 1989, 92). In addition, they need to "see mathematics as an integrated whole" (NCTM 1989, 84) and understand that mathematics is useful and meaningful in their lives outside of the mathematics class.

Students often ask, "Why should I learn fractions?" or "When am I ever going to use this?" While not everything that we learn has implications for direct use in our everyday lives, we should believe that the knowledge is useful and substantive. The best way to motivate students to learn a new skill is to tie it to a broader mathematical strand or to problems from the world outside the classroom. This chapter highlights interesting activities and projects to help students develop a deeper and more meaningful understanding of fractions and decimals—how they are alike and how they are different.

FOLDING A TANGRAM

The "Folding a Tangram" activity connects fractions and geometry in a way that has built-in appeal to students. It allows them to "experience" the size of each shape, both spatially and symbolically, and encourages them to follow oral directions.

"Tangram Thinkers," a problem-solving activity, permits students to use their newly created tangram pieces to construct polygons. By working in pairs, students develop their interpersonal intelligence while solving a problem that nourishes their visual/spatial intelligence.

MAKING A TANGRAM QUILT

The "Making a Tangram Quilt" project uses the tangram pieces produced in the "Folding a Tangram" activity to design quilt squares that will eventually become a part of a class quilt. Each student begins by designing his or her own tangram quilt square and analyzing it to compute the fractional part of the whole each color represents. Finally, the fraction is converted to a percent. Students, now working in pairs, choose the design they like best and problem-solve to transfer the design; this square represents their contribution to the class quilt. The "Making a Tangram Quilt" project takes students through the real-life process of producing a quilt—from creating the pieces to designing the squares, and, finally, to creating the quilt. What begins as a simple fraction activity becomes a "work of art."

DESSERT FOR A CROWD

This activity uses an actual recipe for a devil's food cake with marshmallow frosting. The original recipe serves eight people. The students, working together, change the recipe to bake enough cakes to feed their math class (or perhaps all of the students in the school). What happens if you need $4\frac{1}{2}$ eggs? Or $6\frac{2}{3}$ cakes? If you have a kitchen the students can use, perhaps you might want to bake the cakes for a special occasion!

5 X 5 PUZZLE CENTS

"5 x 5 Puzzle Cents" is a puzzle that makes practice with addition of decimals an entertaining activity. Students are able to manipulate "coins" by cutting out the squares at the bottom of the page. This type of activity encourages students to develop their mathematical reasoning.

CHOCOLATE CHIP COOKIES

In this activity, the cost of each ingredient is listed and students are asked to find the cost of each cookie, how much profit could be made if they were sold, and what percent the profit represents. The next best thing to eating these cookies is thinking about eating them!

MUSIC AND FRACTIONS

Students can make connections between mathematics and music by exploring the rhythmic value of each note and using these values to complete measures of a song. Students utilize their fractions skills in this "real-world" activity. Other activities have students "adding" and "subtracting" notes. While the activities are designed to have students employ a mathematical skill, they also communicate an authentic application of the use of fractions in everyday life.

MATHEMATICAL PALINDROMES

Palindromes have played a fascinating role in language as well as mathematics. They can be words, numbers, or even musical notes. Words such as "racecar," "reviver," and "rotator" can be written the same backward and forward. A famous palindrome, "A man, a plan, a canal—Panama!," is the epitaph of Ferdinand de Lesseps, who was associated with the famous canal. We even have whole sentences, such as an amazing one written in 1967 by James Michie, "Doc note, I dissent. A fast never prevents a fatness. I diet on cod." There are even tongue-twisters, such as Leigh Mercer's: "Top steps pup's pet spot."

An interesting palindromic poem was written by J. A. Lindon,

> As I was passing near the jail,
> I met a man but hurried by.
> His face was ghastly, grimly pale.
> He had a gun. I wondered why
> He had a gun. I wondered why,
> His face was ghastly! Grimly pale,
> I met a man, but hurried by;
> As I was passing near the jail.

There are also palindromic numbers; they are the same whether they are read from left to right or right to left. An example of a palindromic number is 123321. The "Mathematical Palindromes" worksheet gives students an opportunity to experiment with a technique that usually produces a palindromic number while they practice addition and collect some data for future discussion and analysis.

"Music and Palindromes" extends students' newly learned knowledge of music to a more creative realm—that of music writing. But this is music writing with a little twist! The example shown is a musical piece that contains a palindromic sequence. Students are given the opportunity to create their own musical masterpieces in this manner.

All of the activities and puzzles in this chapter are aimed at enticing students to learn fractions and decimals by appealing to their different interests, varying abilities, and novel learning styles, while furthering the growth of their multiple intelligences. A new way to look at an old but very important topic!

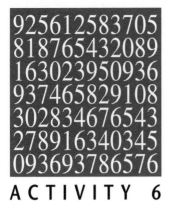

Folding a Tangram

MATH TOPICS

informal geometry, oral directions, mathematical connections

TYPES OF INTELLIGENCES

logical/mathematical, visual/spatial, verbal/linguistic, bodily/kinesthetic, intrapersonal

---

CONCEPTS

Students will do the following:

1. Follow oral directions to fold a paper tangram

2. Use their tangram pieces to visualize shapes and areas of polygons

3. Informally understand geometric terms and the attribute of shapes

4. Use their tangram pieces to solve problems and design a quilt square

---

MATERIALS

one sheet of 8¹/₂ x 11 inch paper for each student; scissors; "Folding a Tangram" worksheets; "Tangram Thinkers" worksheets

WHAT TO DO

Give each student a sheet of paper and a pair of scissors. As you give directions and demonstrate, focus on the following:

1. The names of the polygons formed (When folding isosceles right triangles, right trapezoids, squares, and parallelograms are formed.)

2. The areas of each of the shapes (if the original square equals 1)

3. Which of the polygons are congruent; which are similar (the right triangles are similar)

4. The attributes of each polygon

5. The difference between congruence and similarity

6. What fractional part each tangram piece is of the whole square

"Tangram Thinkers," an extension that follows the folding activity, asks students to work in pairs and use their tangram pieces to solve puzzles that emphasize visual/spatial intelligence.

VARIATION

Students can find the perimeter of triangles using the Pythagorean Theorem.

ASSESSMENT

1. Student observation

2. Grading matrix

3. Journal question: "Describe the attributes of each of the polygons formed during the tangram activity."

Folding a Tangram
Worksheet

Directions: Listen to and watch your teacher's demonstration. You can follow along with these written directions.

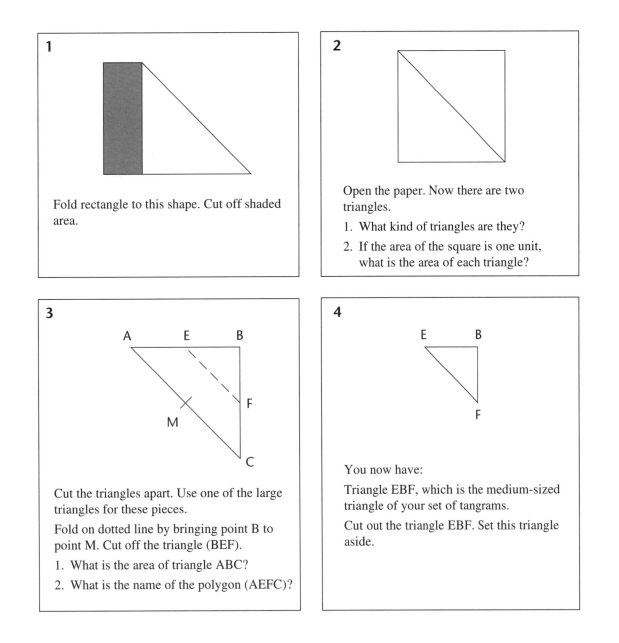

1

Fold rectangle to this shape. Cut off shaded area.

2

Open the paper. Now there are two triangles.

1. What kind of triangles are they?
2. If the area of the square is one unit, what is the area of each triangle?

3

Cut the triangles apart. Use one of the large triangles for these pieces.

Fold on dotted line by bringing point B to point M. Cut off the triangle (BEF).

1. What is the area of triangle ABC?
2. What is the name of the polygon (AEFC)?

4

You now have:

Triangle EBF, which is the medium-sized triangle of your set of tangrams.

Cut out the triangle EBF. Set this triangle aside.

Folding a Tangram—Worksheet (Continued)

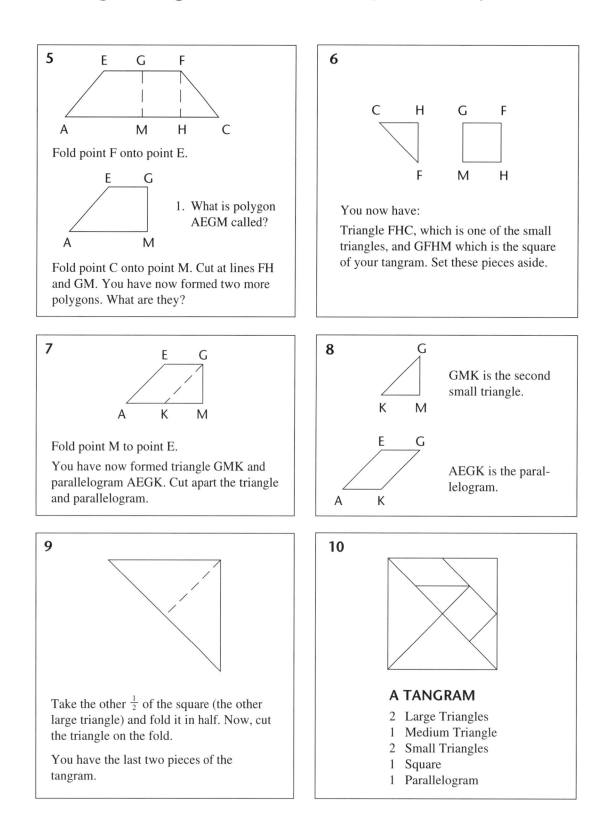

5

Fold point F onto point E.

1. What is polygon AEGM called?

Fold point C onto point M. Cut at lines FH and GM. You have now formed two more polygons. What are they?

6

You now have:

Triangle FHC, which is one of the small triangles, and GFHM which is the square of your tangram. Set these pieces aside.

7

Fold point M to point E.

You have now formed triangle GMK and parallelogram AEGK. Cut apart the triangle and parallelogram.

8

GMK is the second small triangle.

AEGK is the parallelogram.

9

Take the other $\frac{1}{2}$ of the square (the other large triangle) and fold it in half. Now, cut the triangle on the fold.

You have the last two pieces of the tangram.

10

A TANGRAM

2 Large Triangles
1 Medium Triangle
2 Small Triangles
1 Square
1 Parallelogram

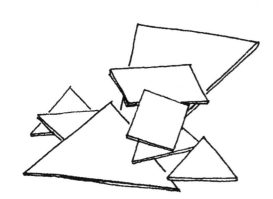

Folding a Tangram
Grading Matrix

Names _____

_____

_____

_____

Date _____   Class _____

Criteria	4	3	2	1
Ability to follow oral directions				
Quality of completed tangram				
Journal description of polygons				

Comments:

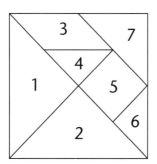

Tangram Thinkers
Worksheet

Names _____

Date _____   Class _____

Work with a partner and use your tangram pieces to see how many different ways, if any, you can form these figures. You can describe the combinations of pieces you use by using the numbers assigned to each in the diagram above.

Number of pieces you can use to form a:	Square	Rectangle	Triangle	Trapezoid	Parallelogram
1					
2					
3					
4					
5					
6					
7					

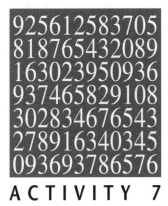

Making a Tangram Quilt

MATH TOPICS

fractions, decimals, percents, problem solving, geometry, connections

---

TYPES OF INTELLIGENCES

visual/spatial, logical/mathematical, verbal/linguistic, interpersonal

---

CONCEPTS

Students will:

1. Use tangram pieces to design a quilt square with a partner

2. Problem-solve a means to copy their design to an 8 x 8 grid that is a different size than the square designed with the tangram pieces

3. Calculate the number, fractional part, and percent each color used in their design represents of the whole square

4. Transfer the design representing the best work of the pair to an 8 x 8 grid

---

MATERIALS

tangram pieces from the tangram activity; copies of "Making a Tangram Quilt" worksheets 1 and 2; crayons, colored pencils, or markers; an 8 x 8 grid for students to transpose their designs (this can be used as the final design if you are going to make a paper quilt. Note: to make grids that are 8 x 8 inches, cut them from a roll of 1-inch grid paper.); fabric crayons for designing the actual quilt square (if you do not intend to make a fabric quilt, these are not necessary)

WHAT TO DO

Discuss with the students how they should go about designing, in pairs, a square using their tangram pieces. It is important they understand that they should not plan to use all seven pieces and may reuse shapes to complete a pleasant design. For example, a quilt square could be made with only small triangles and squares or with the two large triangles and combinations of small triangles and parallelograms. There is a great deal of mathematics in this lesson! For students to design a quilt square with no overlapping pieces and no gaps, the pieces or parts of the square must add up to $^{64}/_{64}$, 1, or 100%.

A paper quilt can be made by forming a rectangular array of the squares produced by the pairs of students. A 3 x 4 quilt represents 24 students; a 4 x 5 quilt represents 40 students.

If you decide to make a fabric quilt, designs must be drawn with fabric crayons, following the directions on the crayon box. (You can find the nearest location selling fabric crayons by calling 1-800-CRAYOLA.) Cut the fabric with $^1/_4$ inch seam allowance on each side of the square to allow sewing.

You can design your quilt in a number of ways. Here is an example of an interesting quilt design:

2" square

8" x 2" rectangle

8" square

To sew, pieces need $^1/_4$" seam allowance on each side.

VARIATION

While this activity works well as designed, it is possible for students to actually sew a quilt using fabric. If this is done, students need to do the following:

1. Cut out pieces of an 8 x 8 grid

2. Make pattern pieces to cut the fabric (these need a $1/4$-inch seam allowance cut on each edge of the pattern piece)

3. Measure a $1/4$-inch seam line and carefully sew on this line

ASSESSMENT

1. Student observation

2. Grading matrix

3. Journal questions:

   a. "What fractional part of your tangram is the large triangle? The medium triangle? The small triangle? The square? The parallelogram? Explain your answer."

   b. "Which of your tangram pieces have the same area? The same perimeter? Explain your answer."

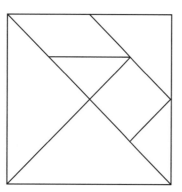

Making a Tangram Quilt
Worksheet 1

Names of Designers _____

Date _____ Class _____

Directions: Use your tangram pieces to design a quilt square, then copy the design onto an 8" x 8" grid. Your tangram pieces are bigger than the grid below, so you will need to analyze the design and copy it carefully. Be sure that each section is colored in (any spaces will be holes in the quilt.) Be sure to use fabric crayons to color in the design as dark as you can. When you are finished, the design will be ironed on an $8\frac{1}{2}$" x $8\frac{1}{2}$" piece of fabric. Each person must design his or her own quilt square and complete the table on the next page to explain the part each color represents in the square.

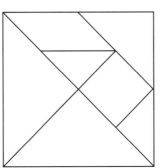

Making a Tangram Quilt
Worksheet 2

Names _____

_____

Date _____   Class _____

COLOR	Number of Squares	Fraction of the Square	Percent of the Square
TOTALS			

In the space provided below, describe the following: (1) how you calculated the fraction of the quilt in each color, and (2) how you converted that fraction into a percent.

_____

_____

_____

_____

_____

What are all of your totals equivalent to? _____

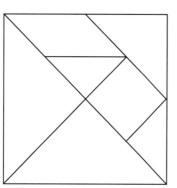

Making a Tangram Quilt
Grading Matrix

Names _____

_____

_____

_____

Date _____   Class _____

Criteria	4	3	2	1
Quality of quilt design. Is it symmetrical? Does it show ingenuity and creativity?				
Problem solving—fractions and percents				
The descriptive paragraph is well done; it clearly describes the thoughts that went into figuring out the fraction and percent each color represents on the quilt.				
How well partners worked together				
Comments:				

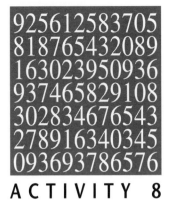

Dessert for a Crowd

MATH TOPICS

fractions, problem-solving, connections

TYPES OF INTELLIGENCES

logical/mathematical, interpersonal, verbal/linguistic

CONCEPTS

Students will do the following:

1. Work with a partner to solve an open-ended problem

2. Convert a recipe to feed a larger number of people

MATERIALS

"Dessert for a Crowd" worksheets

WHAT TO DO

Discuss with students the original recipe. Read the directions with them and make sure they understand appropriate measurements (for example, can you have $\frac{1}{2}$ an egg?). Place the students into pairs and have them convert the recipe and directions to feed the entire mathematics class.

VARIATION

This recipe can be enlarged to feed the entire grade level or the entire school. The calculations become more difficult as the number of people to be fed is enlarged.

ASSESSMENT

1. Observation of student pairs

2. Grading matrix

3. Journal questions:

   a. "Explain the procedures (strategies) you used to enlarge the recipe to feed the entire class."

   b. "How do you think your strategies would have changed if you needed to convert the recipe to feed four people instead of eight?"

Dessert for a Crowd
Worksheet 1

Directions: The recipe for devil's food cake with marshmallow frosting will serve about eight people (each person will get $\frac{1}{8}$ of the cake). Work with your partner to alter the recipe so that you can make enough cakes to feed the class. Be sure to rewrite the directions so that you will be making the correct number of cakes.

Devil's Food Cake

$\frac{1}{2}$ cup margarine	2 cups flour
$1\frac{1}{2}$ cups sugar	1 teaspoon baking soda
1 egg	$\frac{3}{4}$ teaspoon salt
2 egg yolks	1 cup milk
3 ounces unsweetened chocolate, melted and cooled	1 teaspoon vanilla extract

Cream butter. Gradually add sugar and cream until light and fluffy. Add egg and egg yolks, one at a time, beating well after each addition. Add chocolate. Add dry ingredients alternately with milk. Add vanilla. Pour into two round 9-inch layer pans. Bake in a 350° oven for about 30 minutes. Cool and frost with marshmallow frosting.

Marshmallow Frosting

$1\frac{1}{2}$ cups sugar	$1\frac{1}{2}$ teaspoons corn syrup
$\frac{1}{3}$ cup water	1 teaspoon vanilla extract
$\frac{1}{4}$ teaspoon salt	16 ($\frac{1}{4}$ pound) marshmallows, quartered
2 egg whites	

Combine all of the ingredients, except vanilla and marshmallows, in the top part of a double boiler. Beat for 7 minutes, or until stiff peaks form. Remove from heat and add vanilla and marshmallows.

Dessert for a Crowd
Worksheet 2

Names _____

_____

Date _____ Class _____

Directions: Work with your partner to figure out the correct quantities of ingredients for this class. Make sure you have enough for every student and a piece for the teacher! Use the spaces provided to design your recipes.

Devil's Food Cake

_____ cup margarine   _____ cups flour

_____ cups sugar   _____ teaspoon baking soda

_____ egg   _____ teaspoon salt

_____ egg yolks   _____ cup milk

_____ ounces unsweetened chocolate,   _____ teaspoon vanilla extract

_____ melted and cooled

Cream butter. Gradually add sugar and cream until light and fluffy. Add eggs and egg yolks, one at a time, beating well after each addition. Add chocolate. Add dry ingredients alternately with milk. Add vanilla. Pour into _____ round 9-inch layer pans. Bake in a 350° oven for about 30 minutes. Cool and frost with marshmallow frosting.

Marshmallow Frosting

_____ cups sugar   _____ teaspoons corn syrup

_____ cup water   _____ teaspoon vanilla extract

_____ teaspoon salt   _____ (_____ pound)

_____ egg whites   marshmallows, quartered

Combine all of the ingredients, except vanilla and marshmallows, in the top part of a double boiler. Beat for 7 minutes, or until stiff peaks form. Remove from heat and add vanilla and marshmallows.

Dessert for a Crowd
Grading Matrix

Names _____

_____

_____

_____

Date _____   Class _____

Criteria	4	3	2	1
Students converted the recipe and directions				
How well students worked together				
Journal description of their solutions				
Comments:				

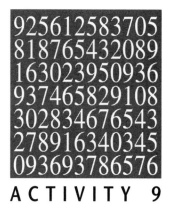

5 x 5 Puzzle Cents

MATH TOPICS

decimals, problem-solving

TYPES OF INTELLIGENCES

logical/mathematical, bodily/kinesthetic, intrapersonal, verbal/linguistic

---

CONCEPTS

Students will do the following:

1. Use decimal skills to solve problems

2. Work to find multiple solutions

MATERIALS

scissors; "5 x 5 Puzzle Cents" worksheets; calculators (if necessary)

WHAT TO DO

Students can work alone or in pairs. After cutting out the coins on the bottom of the page, allow students time to solve the puzzle. By moving around the tokens, students will find it easier to try different possibilities. Sums give a clue to the

---

numbers that belong in the blanks. A possible solution is shown below.

10¢	5¢	50¢	25¢	25¢
10¢	5¢	5¢	10¢	10¢
5¢	25¢	1¢	25¢	25¢
50¢	10¢	50¢	5¢	50¢
1¢	50¢	1¢	1¢	1¢

VARIATION

Students may be given the option of using calculators to solve the puzzle. Have students create their own puzzle for the rest of the class.

ASSESSMENT

1. Observation of student(s)

2. Grading matrix

3. Journal question: "Explain whether the sums at the end of the rows helped you solve the problem."

5 x 5 Puzzle
Cents
Worksheet

Name(s) _____

Date _____ Class _____

Placing one coin in each square, arrange five pennies, five nickels, five dimes, five quarters, and five half-dollars in this 5 x 5 grid so that the totals in each row and column equal the amount to the right of each row and under each column.

					$1.15
					$.40
					$.81
					$1.65
					$.54
$.76	$.95	$1.07	$.66	$1.11	

5x5 Puzzle Cents—Worksheet (Continued)

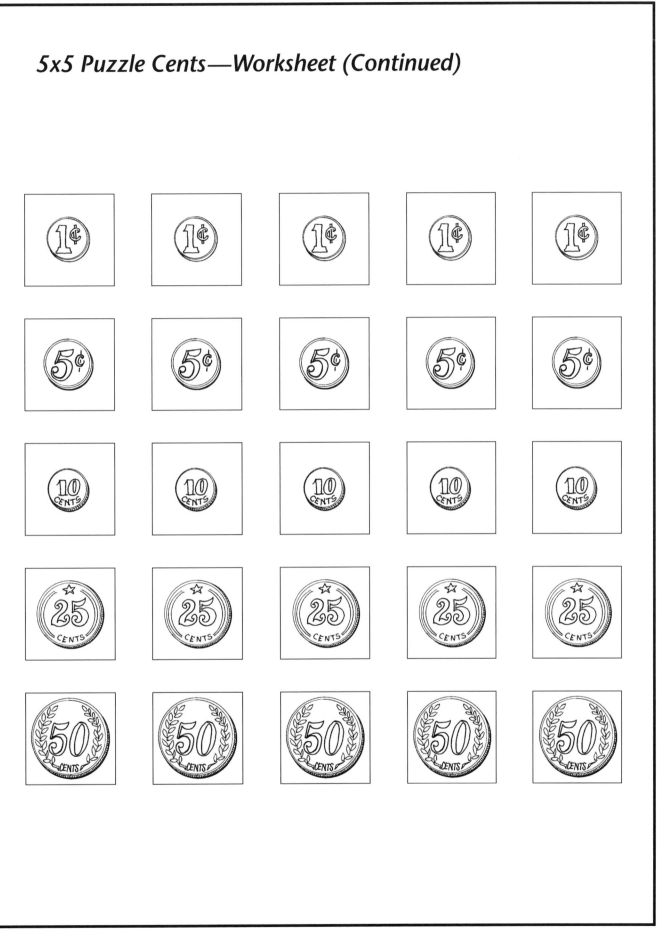

5 x 5 Puzzle
Cents
Grading Matrix

Names _____

_____

_____

_____

Date _____ Class _____

Criteria	4	3	2	1
Students found at least one solution				
How well students worked together (if applicable)				
Journal description of solution				
Comments:				

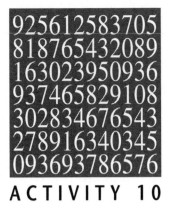

ACTIVITY 10

Chocolate Chip Cookies

MATH TOPICS

computation, problem solving, fractions, decimals, connections

---

TYPES OF INTELLIGENCES

logical/mathematical, interpersonal, verbal/linguistic

CONCEPTS

Students will do the following:

1. Compute the total cost of each of the ingredients

2. Compute the total cost of the cookie batter

3. Compute the cost of one cookie

4. Compute the profit and percent of profit

MATERIALS

"Chocolate Chip Cookies" worksheets; calculators

WHAT TO DO

After students have had a chance to examine the worksheet, discuss the problem and why it is important to find the total cost of each of the ingredients in a recipe, regardless of the quantity needed. Students may need assistance in converting fractions to decimals and interpreting the answers. The cost of baking soda and salt is less than 1¢; this may pose difficulties for some students. The problems are difficult to solve because they combine the multiplication of fractions and decimals. In the first problem, students are asked to multiply the mixed number $4\frac{1}{2}$ by the decimal .32. While it is possible for students to change the 32¢ to a fraction, they will most likely want to change the $\frac{1}{2}$ to 0.5.

Have students work in groups. After they find the total cost for each ingredient, they are asked to find the cost per cookie. If the cookies sell for 50¢ a piece, the profit is about 300%.

VARIATION

Consumerism issues (i.e., percent of profit) may be of great interest to students at this level. Interesting problems involve finding the cost per pound of cosmetics, perfume, or other very highly priced items.

ASSESSMENT

1. Grading matrix

2. Journal questions:

   a. "Explain how there can be a percent greater than 100%. Give an example."

   b. "What would happen if a 25¢ cookie was sold for the price in your example?"

Chocolate Chip Cookies
Worksheet

Names _____

_____

Date _____   Class _____

Ingredient	Amount Needed for Recipe	Cost per unit	Total cost for each item
Margarine	$4\frac{1}{2}$ lbs.	$0.32/lb.	
Creamed Shortening	$4\frac{1}{2}$ lbs.	$0.48/lb.	
White Sugar	$8\frac{1}{2}$ lbs.	$0.31/lb.	
Brown Sugar	7 lbs.	$1.01/lb.	
Eggs	40	$0.08/ea.	
Vanilla (imitation)	$\frac{1}{2}$ cup	$0.40/cup	
Flour	16 lbs.	$0.15/lb.	
Baking Soda	6 Tbls.	$0.013/Tbls.	
Salt	6 Tbls.	$0.0017/Tbls.	
Chocolate Chips	9 lbs.	$2.56/lb.	
TOTAL COST			

TOTAL AMOUNT OF COOKIES: 240 at a cost of _____ ea.

If the cookies are sold at 50¢ each, how much profit would be made? _____

What is the percent of profit? _____

Chocolate Chip Cookies
Grading Matrix

Names _____

_____

_____

_____

Date _____   Class _____

Criteria	4	3	2	1
Correctness of computation (costs)				
How well group worked together				
Journal description of strategies				

Comments:

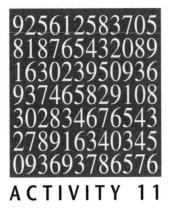

ACTIVITY 11

Music and Fractions

MATH TOPICS

fraction concepts, problem solving, connections

TYPES OF INTELLIGENCES

musical/rhythmic, logical/mathematical, interpersonal, verbal/linguistic

---

CONCEPTS

Students will do the following:

1. Learn the value of musical notes and rests

2. Add fractions to complete the value of measures

3. Subtract fractions to find the difference in the value of notes

4. Complete the value of measures by filling in missing notes and rests

5. Make connections between music and mathematics

MATERIALS

"Music and Fractions" worksheets

WHAT TO DO

The first sheet explains how music is written and that a "$\frac{4}{4}$" in the signature indicates that each measure contains four beats and a $\frac{1}{4}$ note is given one beat. Any combination of notes can be used to add up to four beats. A whole note is worth four beats, a half note is worth two beats, a quarter note is worth one beat, an eighth note is worth one-half a beat, etc. The notes look like this:

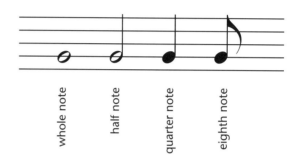

VARIATION

Students should be encouraged to develop their own "fill-in-the-note" activities.

ASSESSMENT

1. Student observation

2. Grading matrix

3. Journal question: "Describe what fractions and music have in common. Explain your answer."

Music and Fractions

Worksheet 1

Names _____

_____

Date _____   Class _____

The music at the right is written in "four-four time," meaning that a quarter note counts as one beat and there are four beats to a measure. Each of the notes pictured is a quarter note; $\frac{1}{4} + \frac{1}{4} + \frac{1}{4} + \frac{1}{4} = \frac{4}{4} = 1$. In each measure of a piece of music, the sum of all of the notes will always equal one! Can you believe it? There are fractions even in music! Look at the explanation of the notes below. It shows you what the notes look like and how much they are worth. A dotted note is equal to the value of the note plus one-half the value of the note (for example, a dotted half note equals $\frac{1}{2} + \frac{1}{4}$, or $\frac{3}{4}$).

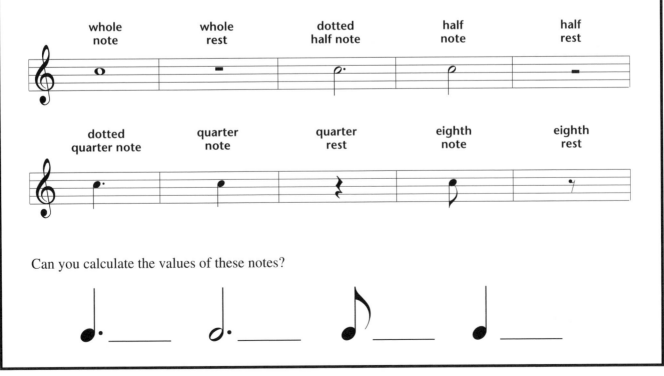

| whole note | whole rest | dotted half note | half note | half rest |

| dotted quarter note | quarter note | quarter rest | eighth note | eighth rest |

Can you calculate the values of these notes?

Music and Fractions

Worksheet 2

Names _____

_____

Date _____   Class _____

Fill in the Note

Each measure of a musical piece has a value of one. The measures written below have something missing—they don't add up to one. For example the first measure contains only two one-fourth notes, meaning the measure has a value of only one-half. Your job is to complete the measure so that it has a value of one by using only one note. You may use the value chart to help you solve these problems.

Fill in the Rest

Sometimes rests (where we count a beat but do not play a note) are used to complete a measure. Complete the following measures by using only one rest.

Music and Fractions
Worksheet 3

Names _____

Date _____ Class _____

Adding Rhythms

Write the answer to each of these addition problems using only one note.

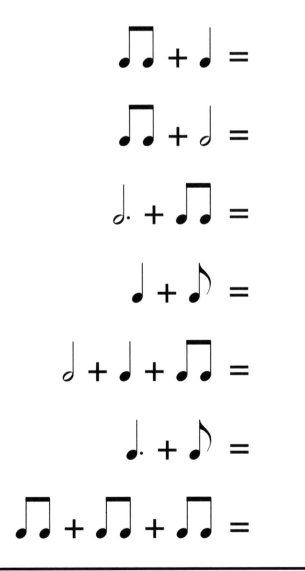

Music and Fractions
Worksheet 4

Names _____

_____

Date _____ Class _____

Subtracting Rhythms

Write the answer to each of these subtraction problems using only one note.

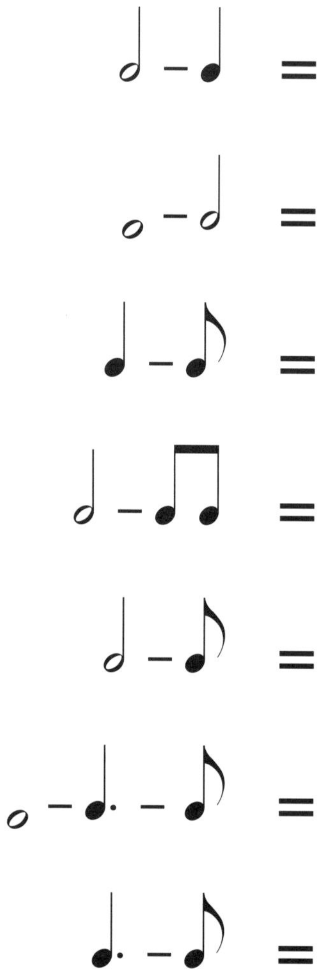

♩ − ♩ =

○ − ♩ =

♩ − ♪ =

♩ − ♫ =

♩ − ♪ =

○ − ♩. − ♪ =

♩. − ♪ =

Music and Fractions
Grading Matrix

Names _____

_____

_____

_____

Date _____   Class _____

Criteria	4	3	2	1
"Fill in the Note" is done correctly				
"Fill in the Rest" is done correctly				
"Adding Rhythms" is done correctly				
"Subtracting Rhythms" is done correctly				
Journal description of strategies				
Comments:				

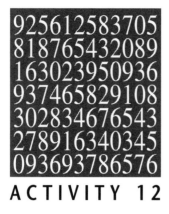

Mathematical Palindromes

MATH TOPICS

computation, problem-solving, data collection

TYPES OF INTELLIGENCES

logical/mathematical, interpersonal, verbal/linguistic, musical/rhythmic

---

CONCEPTS

Students will do the following:

1. Convert numbers into palindromes by following a described procedure

2. Problem-solve to find their own one-step, two-step, and three-step number palindromes

3. Work collaboratively to find a word, phrase, or sentence that is a palindrome

---

MATERIALS

"Mathematical Palindromes" worksheets; markers, crayons, or colored pencils

WHAT TO DO

Discuss with students interesting palindromes from literature. Some sentences and poems are discussed at the beginning of this chapter. Ask students to work in pairs to discover interesting phrases or sentences that are palindromes. Now look at the examples given of number palindromes. Explain the reverse-and-add method of changing numbers into palindromes. Have students choose numbers and use the reverse-and-add method to change them to palindromes.

Give students time to complete the table and the assignment.

VARIATION

You may use the additional sheet, "More Mathematical Palindromes" and have students color-code the grid based on the number of steps it takes to convert numbers to palindromes. Can they find a pattern?

ASSESSMENT

1. Observation of student pairs

2. Grading matrix

3. Journal questions:

   a. "Choose a number and convert it to a palindromic number."

   b. "Why do you think this method works? Explain your reasoning."

Mathematical
Palindromes
Worksheet 1

Names _____

_____

Date _____   Class _____

A palindrome is a word, sentence, or number that is the same forward and backward. "Racecar" and "A man, a plan, a canal—Panama!" are examples of palindromic words and phrases. Write down your own example of a word, sentence, or phrase that is a palindrome: _____

_____

An example of a palindromic number is 1234321. We even have dates that are palindromic, for example, 1881. What will be the first palindromic date in the 21st century? _____

We can turn numbers into palindromes by following some simple arithmetic steps:

1. Write down the original number

2. Reverse the digits

3. Add the original number to the number reversed

If you have a palindrome, you are finished; if you don't, continue the process of reverse-and-add until you have a palindrome. Here are some examples:

38	This is a one-step	156	This is a three-step palindrome.
+ 83	palindrome.	+ 651	
121		807	
		+708	Reverse and add.
		1515	
		+5151	Reverse and add.
		6666	

Mathematical Palindromes—Worksheet 1 (Continued)

There are twenty-four steps to getting a palindrome from the number 89. The palindrome is 8,813,200,023,188. It appears that the number 196 does not have a palindrome. Complete this table:

Number	Number of Steps	Palindrome
148		
59		
364		
352		
85		
785		

Work with your partner to develop one-step, two-step, and three-step palindromes. They are:

one step: _____

two step: _____

three step: _____

More Mathematical Palindromes
Worksheet 2

Names _____

_____

Date _____ Class _____

The table to the right contains the numbers from 10–139. Work with your partner to convert these to palindromes. Follow these directions:

1. If it is already a palindrome, leave it uncolored.
2. If you can convert it into a palindrome in one step, color it yellow.
3. If you need two steps to change it into a palindrome, color it green.
4. If you need three steps to change it into a palindrome, color it red.
5. If you need four or more steps to change it into a palindrome, color it blue.

Do you see a pattern?

Explain: _____

_____

_____

_____

_____

10	11	12	13	14	15	16	17	18	19
20	21	22	23	24	25	26	27	28	29
30	31	32	33	34	35	36	37	38	39
40	41	42	43	44	45	46	47	48	49
50	51	52	53	54	55	56	57	58	59
60	61	62	63	64	65	66	67	68	69
70	71	72	73	74	75	76	77	78	79
80	81	82	83	84	85	86	87	88	89
90	91	92	93	94	95	96	97	98	99
100	101	102	103	104	105	106	107	108	109
110	111	112	113	114	115	116	117	118	119
120	121	122	123	124	125	126	127	128	129
130	131	132	133	134	135	136	137	138	139

What fractional part of your chart is:

1. uncolored? _____

2. yellow? _____

3. green? _____

4. red? _____

5. blue? _____

More Mathematical Palindromes

Grading Matrix

Names _____

_____

_____

_____

Date _____   Class _____

Criteria	4	3	2	1
Table is completed correctly				
How well group worked together				
Examples of palindromes are complete and correct				

Comments:

Music and Palindromes
Worksheet 3

Names _____

_____

Date _____   Class _____

If we can have number palindromes, why can't we have musical palindromes? (A tune that is the same whether we play it forward or backward.) An example of a musical palindrome is below. Notice that the notes for each two measure forms can be played either from right to left or from left to right. The blank musical staffs after the example are for you and your partner to use to form your own musical palindrome.

CHAPTER 3

Geometry:
The Mathematical Window
to Our World

CHAPTER 3

Geometry: The Mathematical Window to Our World

Geometry is the mathematics of shape and form. It is one way we can relate school mathematics to our physical world. The NCTM's standards (1989) state that the study of the geometry of one, two, and three dimensions should (1) help develop spatial sense, (2) encourage students to use geometric models to represent and solve problems, and (3) provide opportunities for students to informally explore geometry to give them a different view of mathematics. We can use three-dimensional models (such as blocks, balls, and cylinders) and two-dimensional models (such as geoboards, drawings, and graph paper) to develop geometry concepts and help students recognize and differentiate between shapes.

The van Hieles' research (Fuys, Geddes, and Tischler 1988) indicates that geometric knowledge progresses through a hierarchy of levels. Children first learn how to recognize the entire shape and then progress to analyze the relevant properties of that shape. Only after they become proficient with this can they progress to see the relationship between different shapes, their similarities and differences.

The activities presented in this chapter give students experiences with hands-on activities that help them develop a formal understanding of identifying, describing, and classifying geometric shapes while experiencing their physical qualities. By folding, measuring, and building geometric models, students discover empirically the properties or rules of a class of both two- and three-dimensional shapes.

PENTOMINOES

The first activity, "Pentominoes," is an informal geometry activity that invites students to use the vocabulary of geometry in a dynamic way while enhancing their visual/spatial intelligence. Students find all the combinations of five tiles that touch side to side. They experience the transformations of rotation and reflection while they problem-solve solutions.

OPEN-TOP BOXES

The "Open-Top Boxes" activity has applications from fifth grade math through calculus. Using scissors and tape, students build and compute the volume of each open-topped box to find the one with the greatest area. While the solution can be found using abstract symbols and formulas, it is possible to approximate a solution by trial and testing.

FOLDING CUBES

A follow-up activity to pentominoes, "Folding Cubes" increases to six the number of tiles students use to build their nets. Hexominoes, as these arrangements are called, become cubes when folded. But can your students find the front, right side, left side, and top if they're given the back and the bottom? This is not as easy as it seems. Activities like this help students develop spatial reasoning and encourage experimentation and collaboration to problem-solve.

EXPLORATIONS WITH CEREAL BOXES

"Explorations with Cereal Boxes" uses a commonly found household item to explore some difficult geometric concepts. Students use rectangular prisms and three-dimensional figures, measure the lengths of the sides, and compute both the surface area and volume. How surprising to find the area (a two-dimensional concept) of a three-dimensional shape! Following this, students explore the cost and nutrional value of cereal. Be sure to keep the cereal boxes because this activity precedes the building of a cereal box from a flat piece of tagboard. Can this be done?

DESIGNING CEREAL BOXES

"Designing Cereal Boxes" encourages groups of students to collaborate in the designing and building of their own cereal boxes—down to the advertising and nutritional information on the side panels. By utilizing a variety of strategies, this activity fosters numerous intelligences and develops mathematical concepts of measurement, geometry, and spatial reasoning.

THE PAINTED CUBE

If you build a 3 x 3 x 3 cube and throw it into a bucket of paint, you have "The Painted Cube." Will all of the faces be covered with paint or will some of them be left unpainted? Using cubes and their spatial imaginations, students look for mathematical patterns to make conjectures.

CUBES THAT GROW

"Cubes That Grow" is another activity that examines both the two-dimensional and three-dimensional qualities of cubes. By exploring the ratio of surface area to volume, students are led to a fascinating discovery. Work along with them to experience it yourself!

The geometry activities contained in this chapter focus on the relationships between squares and cubes. They are designed to enhance spatial visualization and reasoning and allow students the opportunity to explore other avenues and approaches to learning mathematics.

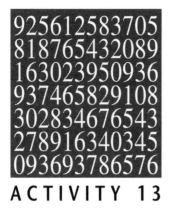

Pentominoes

MATH TOPICS

geometry, measurement, problem-solving, area, perimeter

TYPES OF INTELLIGENCES

visual/spatial, logical/mathematical, interpersonal, verbal/linguistic, bodily/kinesthetic

---

CONCEPTS

Students will do the following:

1. Use a grid to find the twelve different pentominoe pieces

2. Use their pentominoes to solve area problems

3. Experiment with transformations to eliminate duplicate pentominoes

4. Work collaboratively to problem-solve the solutions

MATERIALS

"Pentominoes" worksheets; scissors; markers or colored pencils

WHAT TO DO

Place students into working pairs and give each pair a copy of the "Pentominoes" worksheet. Discuss what "legal" and "illegal" pentominoes are. Legal pentominoes have a side touching; they are not merely joined at a point:

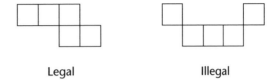

Legal   Illegal

There are twelve different pentominoes. (Students should not be given this information—it is important that they problem-solve and experiment to find them.) Caution the students about rotations and flips. If a pentominoe can be rotated or reflected and look like another, it is not a different pentomino. It is the same one!

The twelve pentominoes are shown below.

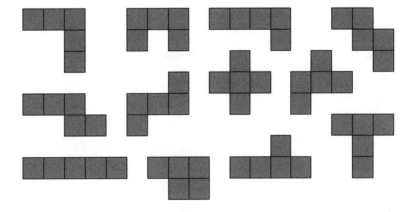

When they are finished, ask the students the following questions:

1. Do all of these pentominoes have the same area?

2. Do they have the same perimeter? Which has the largest perimeter? Which has the smallest?

3. Are any of these quadrilaterals? pentagons? hexagons? octagons? decagons?

VARIATION

Discuss the idea of polyominoes, geometric shapes that are formed by combining squares. For example, monominoes are made of one square, dominoes are formed from two squares, triominoes from three squares, tetrominoes from four, pentominoes from five, hexominoes from six, and so on. Give students centimeter graph paper and have them find the possible arrangements for each type of polyominoe. This table lists the number of arrangements for up to six squares.

Number of Squares	1	2	3	4	5	6
Number of Arrangements	1	1	2	5	12	35

If you have square tiles available, it will be easier for students to find all of the possibilities for larger numbers of squares.

ASSESSMENT

1. Observation of student pairs

2. Student products

3. Grading matrix

4. Journal questions:

   a. "Which of the pentominoes can be folded to form an open box?"

   b. "Do any of the pentominoes display symmetry? Explain your answer with diagrams."

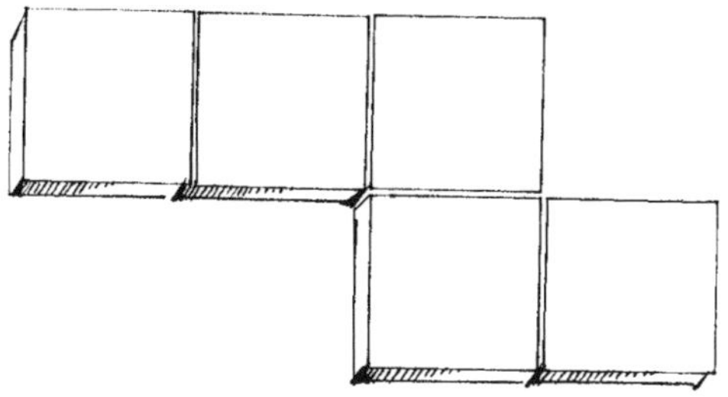

Pentominoes
Worksheet 1

Names _____

Date _____   Class _____

Problem: Arrange five squares into different shapes, following the rule that edges must always be completely touching. Find all possible solutions. Be careful that you do not have congruent shapes that have only been rotated or reflected. Record your solutions on the grid paper below; use colored pencils to make them easier to see.

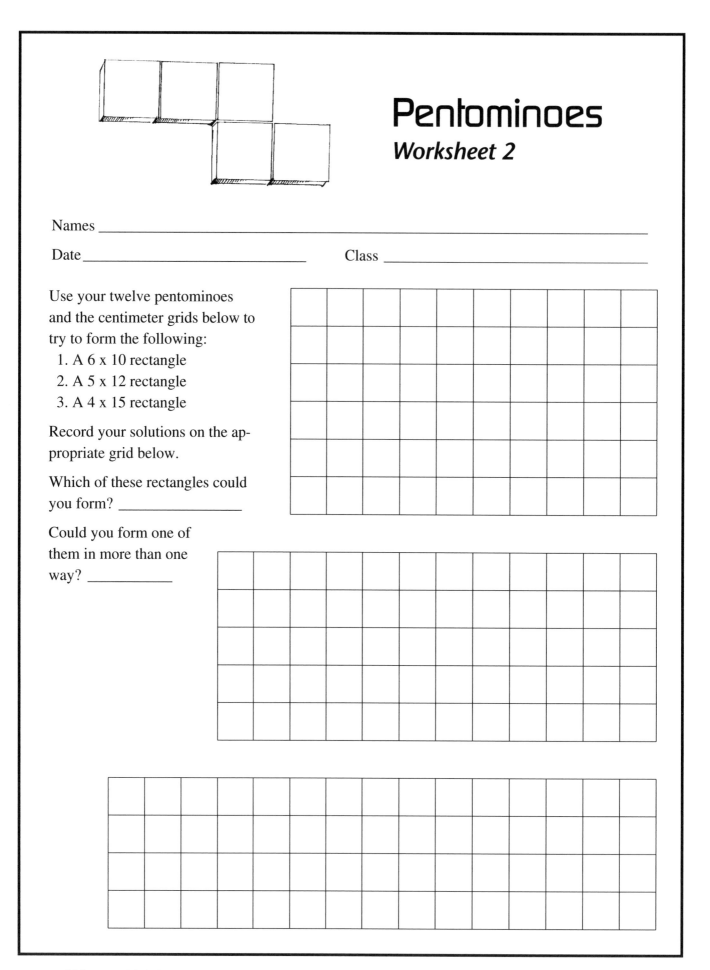

Pentominoes
Worksheet 2

Names _____

Date _____   Class _____

Use your twelve pentominoes and the centimeter grids below to try to form the following:

1. A 6 x 10 rectangle
2. A 5 x 12 rectangle
3. A 4 x 15 rectangle

Record your solutions on the appropriate grid below.

Which of these rectangles could you form? _____

Could you form one of them in more than one way? _____

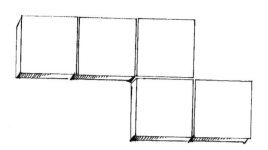

Pentominoes
Worksheet 3

Centimeter Grid Paper

Cut your pentominoes out of this grid.

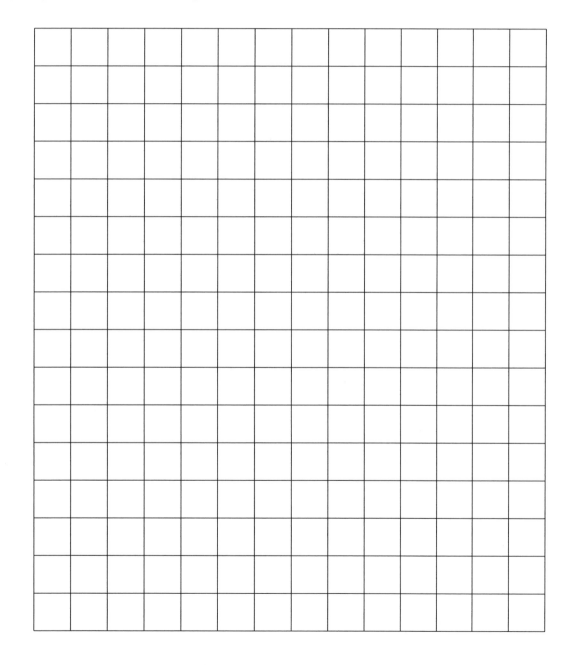

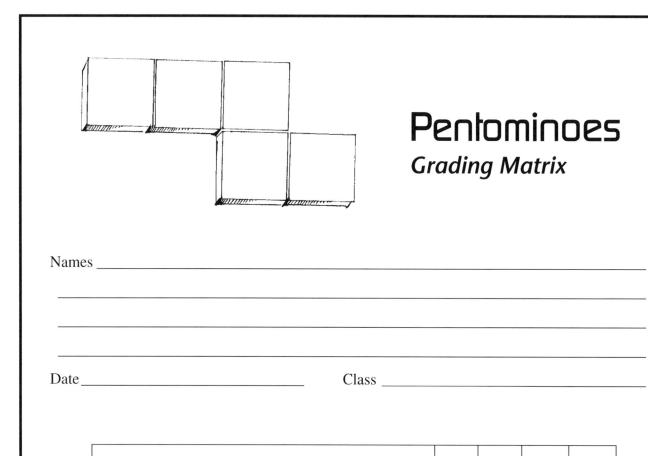

Pentominoes
Grading Matrix

Names _____

_____

_____

_____

Date _____ Class _____

Criteria	4	3	2	1
Number of pentominoes found				
Use of problem-solving strategies				
Each rectangle found				
How well pair worked together				

Comments:

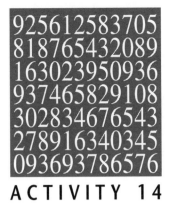

Open-Top Boxes

MATH TOPICS

geometry, data collection, spatial reasoning, problem solving, computation

---

TYPES OF INTELLIGENCES

visual/spatial, logical/mathematical, interpersonal, verbal/linguistic, bodily/kinesthetic

---

CONCEPTS

Students will do the following:

1. Find the open-ended box with the greatest volume

2. Use problem-solving strategies to approach the desired solution

3. Collect and organize data on a table

4. Compute the volume of a rectangular prism

MATERIALS

"Open-Top Boxes" worksheets; scissors; tape; calculators

WHAT TO DO

Use a 17 x 17 grid cutout as a sample to demonstrate how an open-topped box can be formed by cutting a square out of each corner and folding up the sides. The area of the base is now 15 x 15, or 225 square units. To find the volume, multiply the area of the base, 225, by the height, 1. The volume of this box is 225 cubic units. Explain to the students that they will be working to find the box with the greatest volume by decreasing the volume of the base and increasing the height. What happens to the volume?

Have students work in groups of three or four. When students have completed the experiment, discuss the results. Do not be surprised if the box with the greatest volume has a height that is not a whole number length.

VARIATION

Have students find the volumes of boxes with original bases of 15, 16, 18, and 19 and record their findings on the same table to discover if there is a pattern.

ASSESSMENT

1. Student observation

2. Student products

3. Grading matrix

4. Journal questions:

   a. "Explain how you found the box with the greatest volume."

   b. "How do you account for the fact that the box that had the greatest area on its base did not have the greatest volume?"

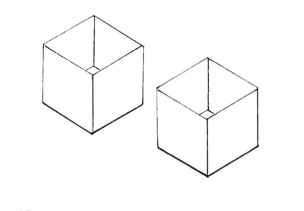

Open-Top Boxes
Worksheet 1

Names _____

Date _____ Class _____

Directions: The 17 x 17 grid on the next page can be made into an open-topped box by cutting squares from each of the four corners and folding up the sides. The volume of a box is found by multiplying the area of its base by its height. Work with your partner to form an open-ended box with the greatest volume, but keep the base a square. Use the table below to find a pattern that might help you solve this problem.

Length of Base	Width of Base	Height of Box	Volume of Box

The dimensions of the box with the greatest volume are: _____

Describe the reasoning you used to solve this problem: _____

_____

_____

_____

_____

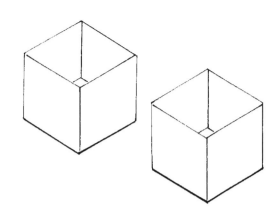

Open-Top Boxes
Worksheet 2

Cut out this grid and use it to help you solve this problem.

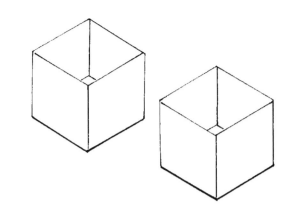

Open-Top Boxes
Grading Matrix

Names _____

_____

_____

_____

Date _____   Class _____

Criteria	4	3	2	1
Quality of solution found				
Use of problem-solving strategies				
Quality and completeness of data table				
How well group worked together				
Comments:				

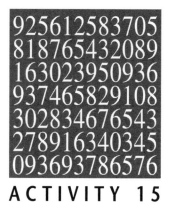

ACTIVITY 15

Classifying Polygons

MATH TOPICS

geometry, spatial reasoning, problem-solving, classification

TYPES OF INTELLIGENCES

naturalist, visual/spatial, logical/mathematical, intrapersonal, verbal/linguistic

---

CONCEPTS

Students will do the following:

1. Understand the attributes of various polygons

2. Use Venn diagrams to classify polygons

3. Understand what each of the sections of the diagram represent

---

MATERIALS

Copy of blackline master for each student

WHAT TO DO

Examine list of polygons with students and discuss the various sections of the 3-Venn circle diagram. Use the following Venn diagram as an example.

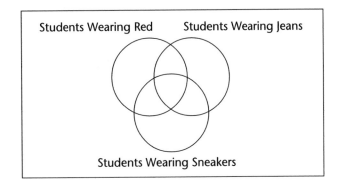

Have students place their initials in the appropriate section. Then ask these types of questions:

1. How many are wearing jeans and something red but are not wearing sneakers?

2. Wearing jeans and sneakers but are not wearing red?

3. Wearing none of these things?

Give the students a copy of the Classifying Polygons worksheet. Have them classify the polygons on the list into the appropriate sections.

Note: The scalene triangle is outside of each of the regions because it has none of the characteristics of the labeled circles. It is not a quadrilateral, has no right angle, and does not have at least two congruent sides.

VARIATION

Have the students develop their own 3-Venn diagrams and a list of other polygons for students to solve.

ASSESSMENT

1. Student observation

2. Student products

3. Grading matrix

4. Journal question: "Explain, in your own words, which polygon(s) could be placed in the very center of the 3-Venn diagram."

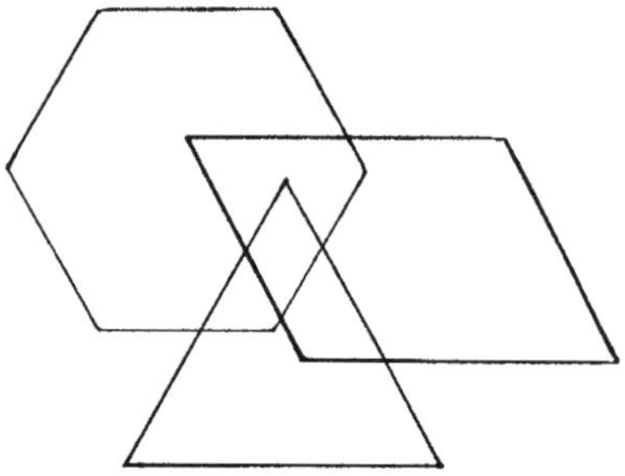

Classifying Polygons
Worksheet

Names _____

Date _____   Class _____

Directions: Analyze the attributes of each shape listed below and place it in the most *accurate* section of the diagram.

rectangle	trapezoid	rhombus	right triangle
square	right trapezoid	isosceles triangle	scalene triangle
regular hexagon	kite	isosceles right triangle	parallelogram

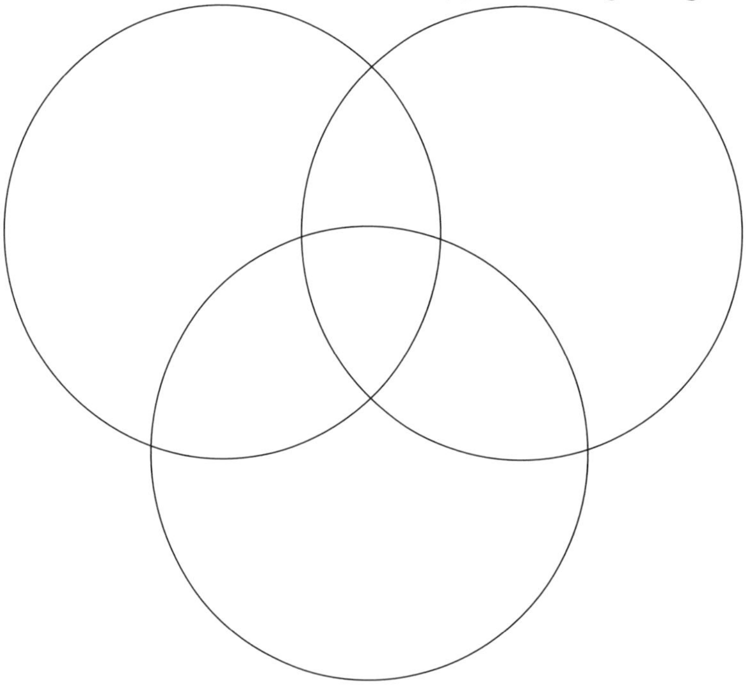

Quadrilaterals　　　　　　　**Polygons with right angles**

Polygons with at least two congruent sides

Explain why you placed each polygon in the section you did. What was it about the attributes of each that helped you decide? _____

_____

_____

_____

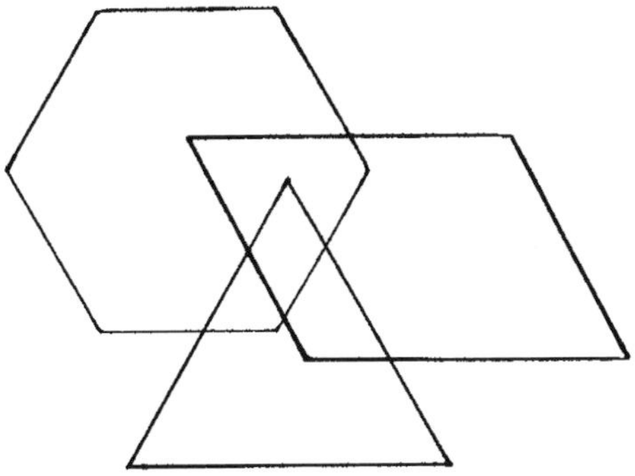

Classifying Polygons
Grading Matrix

Name(s) _____

_____

_____

_____

Date _____   Class _____

Criteria	4	3	2	1
Quality of classification of polygons				
Accuracy of placement				
Written explanation of strategies				

Comments:

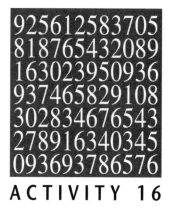

ACTIVITY 16

Explorations with Cereal Boxes

MATH TOPICS

measurement, solid geometry, surface area, volume, computation

---

TYPES OF INTELLIGENCES

visual/spatial, logical/mathematical, interpersonal, verbal/linguistic

---

CONCEPTS

Students will do the following:

1. Analyze the sides of a cereal box (rectangular prism) to find the area of each surface

2. Compute the volume of a rectangular prism

3. Compute whether the box with the largest volume has the greatest weight

4. Compute the cost per ounce (or gram) for each cereal

MATERIALS

cereal boxes; calculators; rulers; "Explorations with Cereal Boxes" worksheets

WHAT TO DO

Hold up a cereal box and ask these questions:

1. What is the difference between the surface area and the volume of this box?

2. What information would we need to find each?

3. Why would we need to know the surface area of an object? Would knowing the surface area help us figure out how much wrapping paper we need to wrap a gift?

4. Explain why we might need to know the volume of a box.

Students generally have a very poor understanding of these two concepts. The exercises in this book are two-dimensional problems that require a three-dimensional solution. To find the surface area, the box can be dissected in the following manner:

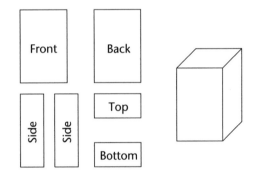

The volume is found by finding the area of the bottom (the base) and multiplying it by the height of the box. By using the box as a manipulative, students can experience the size and measurements required. Have students work in groups of three or four.

VARIATION

Students can find the surface area and volume of other polyhedra.

ASSESSMENT

1. Student observation

2. Student products

3. Grading matrix

4. Journal question: "Explain what you did to find the surface area of your cereal box. How did it differ from finding the volume?"

Explorations with Cereal Boxes
Worksheet 1

Names _____

Date _____   Class _____

Directions: Find four cereal boxes of different sizes and measure the lengths of the sides to find the surface area and volume of each of the boxes. Before you begin, explain the difference between surface area and volume here: _____

_____

_____

_____

Surface Area	Volume (l x w x h)
Name of Cereal: Area of Top: Area of Bottom: Area of Front: Area of Back: Area of Side: Area of Side: Total Surface Area:	
Name of Cereal: Area of Top: Area of Bottom: Area of Front: Area of Back: Area of Side: Area of Side: Total Surface Area:	

Surface Area	Volume (l x w x h)
Name of Cereal: Area of Top: Area of Bottom: Area of Front: Area of Back: Area of Side: Area of Side: Total Surface Area:	
Name of Cereal: Area of Top: Area of Bottom: Area of Front: Area of Back: Area of Side: Area of Side: Total Surface Area:	

Explorations with Cereal Boxes
Worksheet 2

Names _____

Date _____ Class _____

Have you ever wondered which was the best buy in cereal? Is it always the one in the biggest box or the one that costs the least? Now that you've found the surface area and volume of some of these cereal boxes, let's look at what's inside the box—the cereal! Choose ten different cereals and use the table below to list them, figure out their price per ounce, their price per pound, the number of grams of sugar per ounce and per pound, and rank them from 1 to 10, based on the cost (1 is the most expensive; 10 is the least expensive).

Name of Cereal	Price per oz.	Price per lb.	Grams of sugar per oz.	Grams of sugar per lb.	Rank 1–10

Which cereal do you consider to be the healthiest? _____

Why? _____

Is it the best buy? _____

After doing this, which cereal would you buy? _____

Why? _____

Explorations with Cereal Boxes
Grading Matrix

Names _____

_____

_____

_____

Date _____   Class _____

Criteria	4	3	2	1
Surface area computed correctly?				
Volume computed correctly?				
Quality of cereal "investigations"				
How well group worked together				
Comments:				

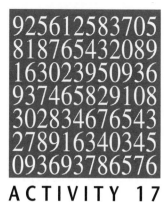

Designing Cereal Boxes

MATH TOPICS

geometry, spatial reasoning, problem solving, measurement

TYPES OF INTELLIGENCES

interpersonal, visual/spatial, logical/mathematical, verbal/linguistic, bodily/kinesthetic

---

CONCEPTS

Students will do the following:

1. Work collaboratively to problem-solve transforming a flat surface into a polyhedron

2. Design a rectangular prism

3. Design the sides of a cereal box to conform to consumer and nutritional issues

---

MATERIALS

1 piece of tagboard (36 cm x 56 cm) for each group of four; scissors; rulers and meter sticks; construction paper; markers, crayons, and colored pencils; glue; calculators and computers (if available for word processing); "Designing Cereal Boxes" worksheets

WHAT TO DO

Discuss with students the hexomino project and how a model of a cube can be made from the net of six squares. Discuss the parts of a cereal box. Examine the dimensions of the front and ask, "When we investigate the top, what dimension must be the same as the front? What does the other dimension stand for?" Have students work in their groups to design and build their cereal boxes.

Precise measurement is very important. Stress to students that the edges and corners of the box must meet—they cannot gap or overlap.

VARIATION

1. Using squares, pentagons, and triangles, students can build other polygons.

2. Students can investigate the Platonic solids (tetrahedrons, cubes, octahedrons, dodecahedrons, and icosahedrons) and construct them.

ASSESSMENT

1. Observation of student groups

2. Student products

3. Grading matrix

4. Journal question: "Explain how an understanding of surface area could help someone design and build a cereal box."

Designing Cereal Boxes
Worksheet

The rules:

1. You have a sheet of poster board that is 36 cm x 56 cm, or 2,016 sq. cm.

2. Your group is charged with designing a rectangular prism (a cereal box) that can be constructed out of a piece of paper the size of the poster board. However, you cannot cut out the pieces. The box needs to be constructed from one piece of paper. Look at these squares:

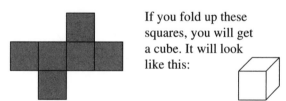

If you fold up these squares, you will get a cube. It will look like this:

3. You must:

   a. Build the box, remembering that a cereal box is made of rectangles, not squares. These rectangles are different sizes. Examine the cereal box to help you with your design.

   b. Design each side of the box to give consumers the following information:

      (1) How much is in the box (weight of the cereal)

      (2) Nutritional information

      (3) Recipes for using the cereal

      (4) Cost

      (5) Any other information normally found on a cereal box

   c. Don't waste your poster board. Use as much of it as possible; any unused board is considered waste. Remember, you have paid for the board that is not used.

4. Each member of your group must be assigned a task and should be responsible for a significant part of the project.

Designing Cereal Boxes
Grading Matrix

Names _____

_____

_____

_____

Date _____   Class _____

Criteria	4	3	2	1
Rectangular prism has utilized the greatest possible surface area of the poster board				
Design of the panels meets the needs of the project				
Quality of the graphic design				
Quality of the nutritional and other panel information				
Cooperative skills of the group				
Comments:				

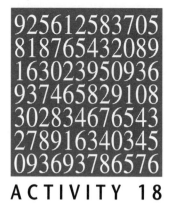

The Painted Cube

MATH TOPICS

geometry, problem-solving, data collection, and analysis

TYPES OF INTELLIGENCES

interpersonal, visual/spatial, logical/mathematical, verbal/linguistic

---

CONCEPTS

Students will do the following:

1. Problem-solve the number of faces that would be "painted" if a 3 x 3 x 3 cube were dropped into a bucket of paint

2. Record their data in a table

3. Analyze the data to describe a pattern

MATERIALS

"The Painted Cube" worksheets; calculators; 27 cubes for pairs of students to use as manipulatives (if possible)

WHAT TO DO

If possible, put together a 2 x 2 x 2 cube so students have a smaller visual model to work from. Go through the questions in the table and discuss the answers with the students. There are relationships between the number of painted faces and the edges, vertices, and faces of the cube. By discovering these patterns, students are able to predict the results of a painted n x n x n cube.

VARIATION

This activity can be adapted for rectangular prisms. What would happen if a cereal box was thrown into a bucket of paint? This is a much more difficult problem.

ASSESSMENT

1. Student observation

2. Student products

3. Grading matrix

4. Journal question: "Discuss the relationship between the number of faces of the cube that are 'painted' and the vertices, faces, and edges of the cube."

The Painted Cube

Worksheet 1

Names _____

Date _____ Class _____

You have a cube that looks like the one on the right, but it's been thrown into a bucket of red paint. The outside is all red, but the inside is not. Use this information to answer the following questions:

How many cubes will have 0 faces (or surfaces) painted red? _____

How many cubes will have 1 face painted red? _____

How many cubes will have 2 faces painted red? _____

How many cubes will have 3 faces painted red? _____

Will any have 4, 5, or 6 faces painted red? Why or why not? _____

_____

Do you think there might be a pattern if the number of cubes that formed the larger cube varied? Let's examine this question and enter the data on the table below.

Size of Cube	Number of Painted Faces			
	0	**1**	**2**	**3**
2 x 2 x 2				
3 x 3 x 3				
4 x 4 x 4				
5 x 5 x 5				
6 x 6 x 6				
n x n x n				

Work with your partner and describe the pattern you see. _____

_____

_____

_____

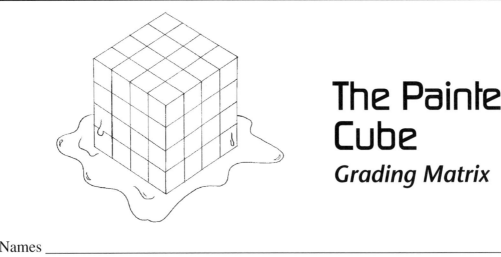

The Painted Cube
Grading Matrix

Names _____

_____

_____

_____

Date _____   Class _____

Criteria	4	3	2	1
Correctly described painted faces				
Accuracy of problem solving in table				
Analysis of problem				
Cooperative skills of pair				

Comments:

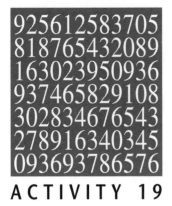

Cubes That Grow

MATH TOPICS

geometry, spatial reasoning, patterns, computation, problem solving, data collection and analysis

---

TYPES OF INTELLIGENCES

logical/mathematical, visual/spatial, interpersonal, verbal/linguistic

---

CONCEPTS

Students will do the following:

1. Use cubes to problem-solve the relationship between their surface area and volume

2. Use collected data to define this relationship for a cube with a side of n units

3. Use formulas to find surface area and volume

MATERIALS

cubes (at least 27 for each pair of students); "Cubes that Grow" worksheets; calculators

WHAT TO DO

Students work with a partner to find the relationship between the surface area and volume of cubes. For a 2 x 2 x 2 cube, the surface area is 4 x 6 = 24. (The number of squares on each side is four and there are six faces.) The volume, however, is $2^3 = 8$. An interesting pattern develops as the area of the base increases because the constant we use to find the surface area is always the area of the base multiplied by 6.

VARIATION

Because of the concrete manipulatives, this activity works well with all grade levels.

ASSESSMENT

1. Student observation

2. Student products

3. Grading matrix

4. Journal question: "At what point is the ratio of surface area to volume equal to 1? When is it less than 1? More than 1? Explain your answers."

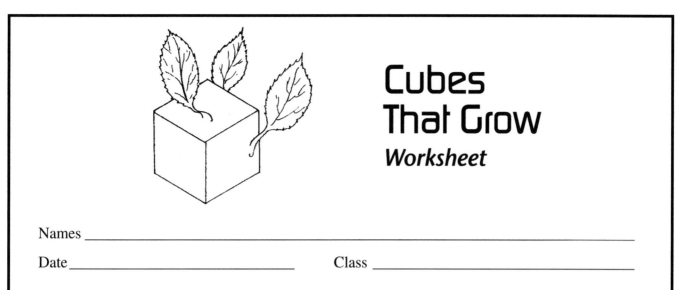

Cubes
That Grow
Worksheet

Names _____

Date _____   Class _____

With identically sized cubes, construct larger cubes with edges of 1, 2, 3, 4, 5, and 6. Complete the table and use the data to find a pattern.

Edge	1	2	3	4	5	6	n
Area of Base	1	4					
Surface Area	6						
Volume	1						
Surface Area / Volume	6/1						

What pattern do you observe? _____

Why do you think this pattern occurs? (Be sure to consider the formula we use to find surface area and the formula we use to find volume.) _____

_____

_____

_____

_____

_____

_____

_____

_____

Cubes
That Grow
Grading Matrix

Names _____

_____

_____

_____

Date _____   Class _____

Criteria	4	3	2	1
Correctly described pattern				
Accuracy of problem solving in table				
Analysis and write-up of problem				
Cooperative skills of pair				

Comments:

CHAPTER 4

The Measure
of Mathematics

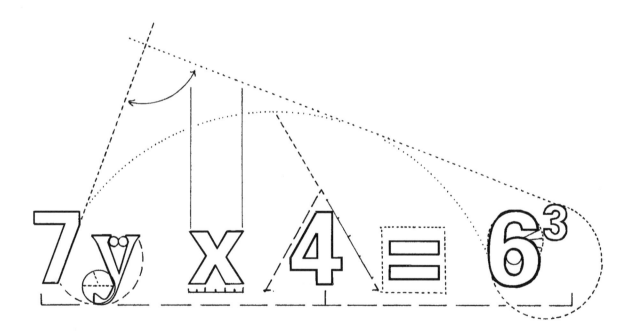

CHAPTER 4

The Measure of Mathematics

In the "real world" we use measurements to answer questions such as "How big is it?" "How long is it?" "How much time does it take?" or "How much does it weigh?" "Do we need an exact number?" "Would an estimate be accurate enough?" To answer these questions, students need "hands-on" experiences that permit them to explore the world around them.

The measure of mathematics consists of more than just measurements of length. Students must understand the concepts of time, weight, and mass. The activities in this chapter are practical applications of mathematics that develop measurement concepts while supporting the multiple intelligences of students.

JUST HOW BIG IS THE STATUE OF LIBERTY?

On Bedloe's Island in New York Bay is one of our country's treasures. It's called the Statue of Liberty and rises more than 306 feet from the bottom of her pedestal to the tip of her torch. Could you figure out how big the Statue of Liberty is if you knew that her arm is 42 feet long? This is the question posed to your students. By taking their own measurements and using ratio and proportion, students will be able to find the size of Lady Liberty. Finally, by designing a scale drawing, they will have approached this problem using their multiple intelligences!

GUMMI WORMS

Edible worms? What's this world coming to? The "Gummi Worms" activity invites your students to describe the physical attributes of a Gummi Worm: what it looks like; the fractional part of each of the colors; how much elasticity it has. By measuring and describing their worms, they are engaging in a rather unconventional view of math.

HOW LONG IS YOUR DIGESTIVE SYSTEM?

Working with a partner and using a twenty-six-foot string, students determine the length of the digestive system. By combining their data, students find a ratio (length of system/ height). Is this a constant? Could this number be used to make predictions of height? This activity creates an interesting data collection that employs measurement and really gets your students involved.

WHAT HAPPENED 1,000,000 SECONDS AGO?

What happened 1,000,000 seconds ago? What's wrong with this question? It's almost as confusing as asking, "How many feet is it from Los Angeles to New York?" We're dealing with extremely inappropriate units of measurement! By converting to normal units, your students will discover some interesting facts.

HOW LONG WOULD IT TAKE TO WALK TO CHINA?

Did anyone ever tell you that if you dug a deep enough hole you would end up in China? What they meant was, if you were to dig through the diameter of the earth, you would dig through to the other side of the globe. That's probably true— but you would be in the Indian Ocean if you started out in the United States. "How Long Would It Take to Walk to China?" is an activity that encourages students to problem- solve how long it would take to walk the diameter of the earth.

BUYING APPLES BY THE POUND

If apples cost 89¢ per pound, how much is one? "Buying Apples by the Pound" is an activity that asks students to predict the cost, graph their predictions, and weigh the apples to find the cost of one. This task combines measurement with some consumer education.

EGGSCETERA

Does it pay to buy jumbo rather than large eggs? Are we getting a better buy because of the larger size? "EggsCetera" is an activity where students measure the circumference, mass, and height of different-sized eggs and use their data to compute the best buy.

To understand the concepts involved with measurement, students must be actively involved in hands-on projects. The activities in this chapter provide these experiences while fostering the multiple intelligences of your students.

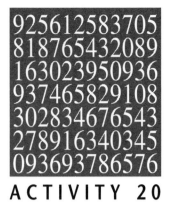

Just How Big Is the Statue of Liberty?

MATH TOPICS

measurement, estimation, ratio, proportion, data collection, analysis, scale drawing, computation

---

TYPES OF INTELLIGENCES

bodily/kinesthetic, logical/mathematical, verbal/linguistic, visual/spatial, intrapersonal, interpersonal

---

CONCEPTS

Students will do the following:

1. Estimate the size of the Statue of Liberty by using ratio and proportion

2. Make suppositions based on data collection and analysis

3. Use ratio and proportion to problem solve

4. Work in cooperative groups to problem solve

MATERIALS

"Just How Big Is the Statue of Liberty?" worksheets; calculators; graph paper

WHAT TO DO

Discuss with students the length of the statue's arm. Take some haphazard measurements and try to estimate how many times larger than life the Statue of Liberty really is.

Place students in groups of four, read the directions on worksheet 1, and have students complete the data collection. Once these averages and an average decimal ratio is found, students can predict the size of the Statue of Liberty.

While students should not be given these measurements, the actual sizes are the following:

Height—152 feet 2 inches

Length of right arm—42 feet

Length of hand—16 feet 5 inches

Length of head—17 feet 3 inches

Width of head—10 feet

Length of neck—10 feet 9 inches

The last phase of the project is the scale drawing of the statue. Graph paper of ¹/₄ inch is supplied. Students must determine the appropriate scale and then design their scale drawings.

VARIATION

Jonathan Swift's *Gulliver's Travels* has an interesting section describing Gulliver's adventures in Lilliput. There are many references to the relative size of Gulliver and the little people. This would make an interesting extension to Lady Liberty.

ASSESSMENT

1. Observation of student groups

2. Scale drawing and student products

3. Grading matrix

4. Journal questions:

   a. "How can ratio and proportion be helpful in estimating the size of large objects?'

   b. "Describe an activity that could be made easier by using ratio and proportion."

Just How Big Is the Statue of Liberty?

Worksheet 1

Names _____

_____

Date _____

Class_____

The Statue of Liberty, on Liberty Island in New York Bay, is one of the largest statues in the world. Liberty rises 306 feet 8 inches from the bottom of her pedestal to the tip of her torch. Designed by Frédéric Auguste Bartholdi, the Statue of Liberty was a gift to the people of the United States from the people of France. Lady Liberty is a very large woman. The length of her right arm is 42 feet! Your group's job is to figure out her remaining dimensions by using ratio and proportion.

Directions: Find the length of the right arm of each member of your group. Then find the average length of the arms. By setting up a ratio, you can compute how many times larger the statue's arm is than your group's average. Use this ratio to find the size of the rest of the statue.

Group Member	Length of Arm	Length of Hand	Height	Width of Head	Length of Head	Length of Neck
AVERAGE						

To find the ratio of the size of the Statue of Liberty's arm to the size of our arm:

$$\frac{42 \text{ feet}}{\text{Group Average (in feet)}} =$$

How many times larger is the Statue of Liberty's arm than the average of your group? _____

_____

Find the decimal ratio for the other parts of the body. What is the average decimal ratio? _____

Just How Big Is the Statue of Liberty?
Worksheet 2

Names _____

_____

Date _____

Class _____

Use the data you collected to estimate the size of the Statue of Liberty. Use the ratio computed by your group as a multiplier. Enter your estimates on the table below.

The average length of our arms		Predicted length of Liberty's arm	
The average length of our hands		Predicted length of Liberty's hand	
Our group's average height		Predicted height of Liberty's hand	
The average width of our heads		Predicted width of Liberty's head	
The average length of our heads		Predicted length of Liberty's head	
The average length of our necks		Predicted length of Liberty's neck	

How many times "larger than life" is the Statue of Liberty? _____

Explain how you got your answer. _____

_____

The Statue of Liberty weighs about 450,000 pounds. If the average woman weighs about 130 pounds, how many times more does the statue weigh than the woman?

_____

How does this ratio compare with the ratios you obtained in the experiment? _____

_____

There is an observation room in the crown of the Statue of Liberty. Forty people can stand in the head. The head is 10 feet wide. Estimate the area of the crown and its circumference. Explain your answer. ___

_____

_____

_____

Just How Big Is the Statue of Liberty?

Worksheet 3

Names _____

Date _____

Class _____

Use this grid to design and draw a scale model of Lady Liberty. This is a $\frac{1}{4}$ " grid.

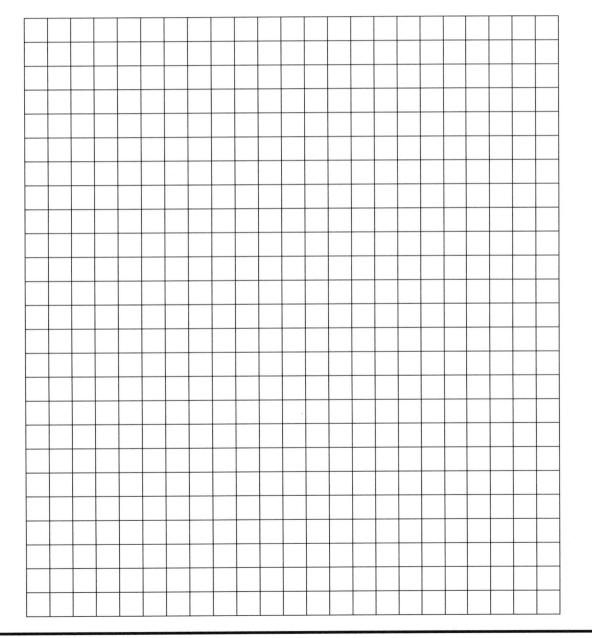

Just How Big Is the Statue of Liberty?

Grading Matrix

Names _____

_____

_____

_____

Date _____

Class _____

Criteria	4	3	2	1
Quality of computation and data collection				
Completeness of explanations (worksheet 2)				
Quality of scale drawing				
How well group worked together				
Comments:				

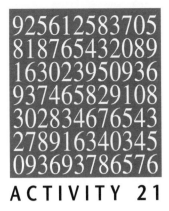

925612583705
818765432089
163023950936
937465829108
302834676543
278916340345
093693786576

ACTIVITY 21

Gummi Worms

MATH TOPICS

measurement, statistics, fractions, percents, graphing, mathematical connections

---

TYPES OF INTELLIGENCES

logical/mathematical, visual/spatial, verbal/linguistic, bodily/kinesthetic, intrapersonal, naturalist

---

CONCEPTS

Students will do the following:

1. Measure to the nearest mm

2. Compute the fractional part of the whole

3. Compute the percent of a whole

4. Experiment with elasticity

5. Analyze data and graph class results

MATERIALS

1 Gummi Worm for each student (or pair of students); copies of "Gummi Worms" worksheet 1; calculators; transparency of "Gummi Worms" worksheet 2

WHAT TO DO

Hold up a Gummi Worm and ask students to describe the physical attributes of the worm. What does it look like? How many different colors does it have? About what fractional part is each color of the whole worm? What percent?

Students can work alone or in pairs on this experiment. Set up groups and give each one a worm and a data collection sheet. When they have completed their data collection, encourage students to draw a picture of their worm and write a brief autobiography about it.

When all the data are collected, have students graph their data on an overhead transparency. They can use the graph to find the mean, median, and mode of the data.

VARIATION

While the Gummi Worm is a nonregular polyhedra, it is possible to find its volume (it is an irregular cylinder) and average mass. In addition, it does have some elasticity. Other everyday items could be examined and the property of elasticity investigated.

ASSESSMENT

1. Student products

2. Grading matrix

3. Journal question: "Explain how a graph could be used to help us find the mean, median, and mode of the data."

Gummi Worms
Worksheet 1

Name(s) _____

Date _____ Class _____

An Experiment in Variation

Directions: Use your Gummi Worm to answer these questions. Measure to the nearest mm. Place your answer in the table below.

Colors	Length of Section				Total Length	Fractional Part of Section				% of Length of Section			
	1	2	3	4		1	2	3	4	1	2	3	4

Now stretch your Gummi Worm as far as it will go, but don't let it break! Now let it go back to its original shape. Remeasure the total length.

The new length is: _____

Did it retract to its initial length?_____

Do you believe from this experiment that your Gummi Worm is elastic? _____

Why or why not? _____

Describe the attributes of your Gummi Worm. What does it smell like? What does it feel like? What do you think it will taste like, etc. _____

_____

_____

_____

In the space below, draw a lifesize model of your Gummi Worm, name it, and tell us something about the life of your Gummi Worm.

Gummi Worms
Worksheet 2

Name(s) _____

Date _____ Class _____

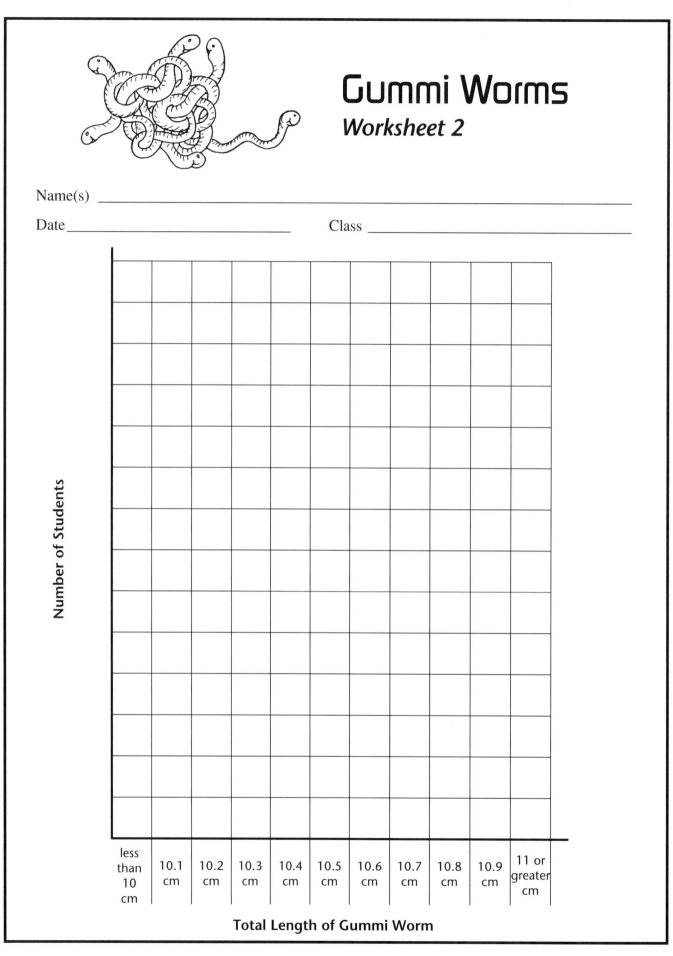

Number of Students (vertical axis label)

less than 10 cm	10.1 cm	10.2 cm	10.3 cm	10.4 cm	10.5 cm	10.6 cm	10.7 cm	10.8 cm	10.9 cm	11 or greater cm

Total Length of Gummi Worm

Gummi Worms
Grading Matrix

Name(s) _____

_____

_____

_____

Date _____   Class _____

Criteria	4	3	2	1
Quality of data collection				
Correctness of computation (fractions and percents)				
Overall quality of written responses and discussions				
Overall quality of experiment				
Comments:				

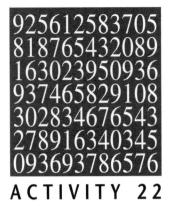

How Long Is Your Digestive System?

MATH TOPICS

measurement, data collections and analysis, mathematical connections

---

TYPES OF INTELLIGENCES

bodily/kinesthetic, verbal/linguistic, logical/mathematical, interpersonal, intrapersonal

---

CONCEPTS

Students will do the following:

1. Work collaboratively to make connections between mathematics and science

2. Measure using a nontraditional instrument and then interpret that distance using a more traditional method

3. Find mean lengths

4. Look for patterns between the length of their digestive systems and total height

---

MATERIALS

string (about 26 feet for each pair); copies of "How Long is Your Digestive System?" worksheet 1; overhead transparency of worksheet 2; meter sticks, yard sticks, or tape measures; calculators

WHAT TO DO

Ask students, "How long do you think your digestive system is? Remember that it starts at the mouth!" Give students a chance to discuss this, write their answers down so they may be referred to at a later time, and then give each group of four students copies of the worksheet. Go over the procedures with them.

Each pair must get the supplies they need and then begin the collection of data. For the class record sheet, you will need the height of each child in the class. Remind students to take a traditional measurement of their height in addition to the other nontraditional measurements.

When individual pairs have finished collecting data, have them write on the class record sheet the mean length and height of the individuals in their group. Place these in ratio form to see if there appears to be a ratio of the length of the students' digestive systems to their height.

VARIATION

This activity makes strong connections between mathematics and science. Other human systems can be examined and their relative size compared to the size of the digestive system.

ASSESSMENT

1. Student observation

2. Student products

3. Grading matrix

4. Journal questions: "What relationship did you find between the length of the digestive systems and the mean height of the students in your class? Do you think this number could be used to predict the height of a person if you knew the length of his or her digestive system? Why or why not?"

How Long Is Your Digestive System?
Worksheet 1

Names of Partners _____

Date _____

Class _____

Directions: Before you begin this activity, measure and record your heights.

Name _____ Height _____

Name _____ Height _____

Now measure each of the lengths asked for in the table below. Use a string and tie knots after you have completed each measurement. (Do not cut the string! Keep measuring from each knot.) Work with your partner; help each other with the measurements and knot tying. After you've measured each length, place that measurement in the correct place on the table. *The total length of the system is the sum of each of the parts.* Round your answer to the nearest centimeter. Find the mean length for each measurement.

Your Name	Mouth to back of jaw (Mouth)	Back of jaw to bottom of sternum (Esophagas)	Thumb to pinkie (stomach)	4 x your height (small intestines)	1 x your height (large intestines)	TOTAL LENGTH OF SYSTEM
Mean Length						

Describe (analyze) your findings: _____

_____

_____

_____

How Long Is Your Digestive System?
Worksheet 2

Pair	Mean Length of Digestive System	Mean Height of Group Members	Ratio: Length of System / Height
MEAN			

Does there appear to be a pattern? Explain your answer.

How Long Is Your Digestive System?
Grading Matrix

Names of Students _____

_____

_____

_____

Date _____   Class _____

Criteria	4	3	2	1
Completeness of measurements				
Correctness of computation				
Quality of written analysis				
How well pair worked together				
Comments:				

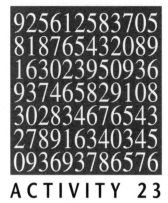

ACTIVITY 23

What Happened 1,000,000 Seconds Ago?

MATH TOPICS

measurement (time), computation, problem solving

TYPES OF INTELLIGENCES

interpersonal, logical/mathematical, verbal/linguistic

CONCEPTS

Students will do the following:

1. Compute length of time using appropriate units

2. Work collaboratively to problem solve a solution

3. Research historical connections

MATERIALS

calculators; "What Happened 1,000,000 Seconds Ago?" worksheets

---

WHAT TO DO

Ask students, "What happened one million seconds ago? Why is this question so difficult to answer? Can we understand the concept of one million seconds ago? Why?" The unit of seconds is inappropriate when the amount of time is so long!

Allow students, working in pairs, time to solve the problem. Then, find out what happened one billion seconds ago—this is one thousand times longer than one million ($1,000,000 = 10^6$; $1,000,000,000 = 10^9$).

1,000,000 seconds is about $11\,^1/_2$ days.

1,000,000,000 seconds is about 32 years.

VARIATION

The next logical extension is to find out what happened one trillion seconds ago, or 10^{12} seconds ago. This was before written history, during prehistoric times. It is an interesting extension to have students explore.

ASSESSMENT

1. Student observation

2. Student products

3. Grading matrix

4. Journal question: "Describe the methods you used to express one million seconds using more appropriate units of measure."

What Happened 1,000,000 Seconds Ago?

Worksheet

Names _____

Date _____ Class _____

We don't usually use seconds to describe really long periods of time. But suppose we did? How long ago was 1,000,000 (1 million) seconds? What were you doing 1,000,000 seconds ago? Work with your partner (and a calculator) to answer this question. Write your answer in the space provided below. _____

_____

_____

Now that you've figured that out, work with your partner to determine how long ago 1,000,000,000 (1 billion) seconds ago was. What was happening 1,000,000,000 seconds ago? What year was it? Were you born? This one may take a little more work. Write your answer in the space provided below. Be sure to use complete sentences and remember that the completeness of your answer counts. _____

_____

_____

_____

_____

_____

What Happened 1,000,000 Seconds Ago?

Grading Matrix

Names _____

_____

_____

_____

Date _____   Class _____

Criteria	4	3	2	1
Correctness of computations				
Quality of written responses				
How well partners worked together				
Comments:				

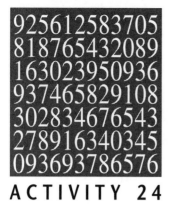

How Long Would It Take to Walk to China?

MATH TOPICS

measurement, data collection and analysis, computation

TYPES OF INTELLIGENCES

bodily/kinesthetic, interpersonal, logical/mathematical, verbal/linguistic, visual/spatial

---

CONCEPTS

Students will do the following:

1. Compute the diameter of the earth

2. Problem solve the speed at which they walk

3. Compute how long it would take them (on average) to walk through the center of the earth

4. Make connections between math and science

5. Work collaboratively to problem solve a solution

MATERIALS

calculators; meter sticks or other measuring instruments; "How Long Would It Take to Walk to China?" worksheets; stopwatches (one for each group of four)

WHAT TO DO

If a globe is available, use it to ask, "If you could walk straight through the earth, do you think you would end up in China?" Students should realize that there is a large body of water on the other side. The problem for this lesson is: "How long would it take to walk through the earth to the other side? To solve this problem, students need to do the following:

1. Determine how quickly they walk. Rate is determined by dividing the distance one travels by the time it takes to get there. In other words, if you travel 10 miles (distance) in 2 hours (time), your rate is 5 mi/hr (rate).

2. Walk a predetermined distance while timing the walk.

3. Divide the distance they walk by the time on the stopwatch to find their rate.

4. Use this rate to compute how long it would take them to walk to the other side of the earth.

VARIATION

This activity combines two measurements—time and distance. Students can compute how long it would take them to walk (a) around the earth (at the equator it's approximately 40,000 km), (b) to the moon (approximately 406,700 km), and (c) across the Pacific Ocean from Panama to Malaysia (approximately 17,700 km).

ASSESSMENT

1. Student observation

2. Student products

3. Grading matrix

4. Journal question: "The United States has over 6,000,000 km of roads. You want to walk across all of them. Explain how you would figure out how long it would take to walk all the roads of the United States."

How Long Would It Take to Walk to China?

Worksheet

Names _____

Date _____

Class _____

If you could walk straight through the earth, do you think you would end up in China? Not if you lived in the United States, you wouldn't! You would be in the middle of the southern portion of the Indian Ocean—not too far (as the crow flies) from Australia.

How long would it take for you to walk there? You need a little bit of information:

> The earth is made of layers, the surface of which is a thin crust about 40 km thick. Under this is a layer of liquid rock called the *mantle,* which is about 2,870 km thick. The mantle surrounds the *outer core* of the center of the earth. Made of liquid iron and nickel, the outer core is about 2,100 km thick. In the center of the earth is the *inner core.* Scientists believe the inner core is a solid ball of iron and nickel that is about 1,370 km to its center. This gets us to the center of the earth!

How far is it from the surface to the center of the earth? _____

How far is it from the surface to the center and back to the surface? _____

Now, let's get to the problem: How long would it take you to walk through the layers of the earth to the center and then back out again to the surface?

Directions: Work with your group to find out how long it would take (as an average) to walk one kilometer. This will help you compute how long it will take you to get from your home to the Indian Ocean by walking the diameter of the earth (right through the middle). Enter your data in the table below.

Name	Distance walked in meters	Time	Rate $R = \dfrac{d}{t}$	Time to walk through the earth (13,480 km)

Explain how your group solved this problem: _____

_____

_____

How Long Would It Take to Walk to China?

Grading Matrix

Names _____

_____

_____

_____

Date _____   Class _____

Criteria	4	3	2	1
Quality of data collection				
Quality of problem-solving strategies				
Analysis and computation				
How well the group worked together				
Comments:				

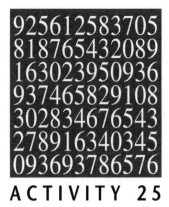

ACTIVITY 25

Buying Apples by the Pound

MATH TOPICS

ratio and proportion, data collection, estimation, computation, rounding decimals, measurement (weight)

TYPES OF INTELLIGENCES

visual/spatial, bodily/kinesthetic, logical/mathematical, interpersonal

---

CONCEPTS

Students will do the following:

1. Estimate the cost of one apple when they are told the price per pound

2. Record their estimates on a table containing a range of prices

3. Weigh the apple to the nearest ounce

4. Compute the cost of one apple

MATERIALS

2 apples of different sizes and weights per group; 1 scale per group of students; overhead transparency of "Buying Apples by the Pound" worksheet 1; copies of worksheets 2 and 3; calculators

WHAT TO DO

Hold up two apples of different sizes. Tell the students that even though the apples shown are different sizes and weights, the cost of each apple is the same—89¢ per pound. Discuss with the students how they might figure out what the cost of one apple would be. Remind students that 16 oz. = 1 lb.

Place students into groups of four and give each group a scale, two apples, and "Buying Apples by the Pound" worksheets. Each apple is weighed and its weight recorded. Have each group compute the cost of each of the apples. Some of the possible strategies for a 6 oz. apple include:

$$\frac{6 \text{ oz.}}{16 \text{ oz.}} = \frac{x¢}{89¢} \quad \text{or} \quad \frac{6 \text{ oz.}}{x} = \frac{16 \text{ oz.}}{89¢} \quad \text{or} \quad \frac{89¢}{16} \times 6$$

This apple, rounded to the nearest cent, costs 33¢. Encourage students to share their strategies with you.

After one of the apples is weighed and costed out, have students estimate the cost of the other apple. If it is larger, will it cost more or less than the smaller apple? Why? Follow the same procedures to weigh and find the cost of the second apple.

ASSESSMENT

1. Observation of student groups

2. Student products

3. Grading matrix

4. Journal question: "Find the cost of one pear if (1) it weighs 7 oz., and (2) one pound of pears costs 68¢. Round to the nearest 1¢ (if necessary). Explain your solution."

Buying Apples by the Pound

Worksheet 1

Directions: One pound of apples this size costs 89¢. How much do you think one apple would cost? Tally your choice in the table below.

My estimate for the cost of one apple:

Cost/Apple	Tally
1¢ – 5¢	
6¢ –10¢	
11¢ – 15¢	
16¢ – 20¢	
21¢ – 25¢	
26¢ – 30¢	
31¢ – 35¢	
36¢ – 40¢	
41¢ – 45¢	
46¢ – 50¢	
Over 50¢	

Buying Apples by the Pound

Worksheet 2

Names _____

Date _____ Class _____

Directions: Use the graph below to record the price predictions of the class. Be sure to label the axes appropriately.

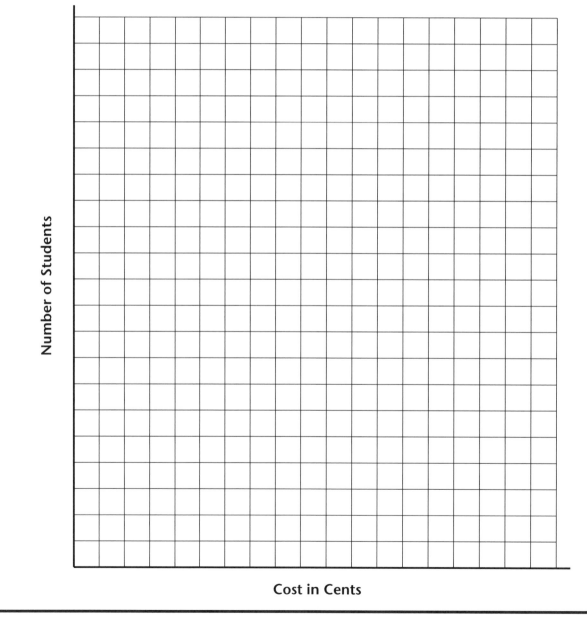

Number of Students (vertical axis)

Cost in Cents (horizontal axis)

Buying Apples by the Pound
Worksheet 3

Names _____

Date _____ Class _____

Directions: Now work with your group to weigh the smaller of the two apples. If these apples sell for 89¢ a pound, compute the cost of one. Do the same for the larger apple. Use the table below to enter the data.

Apple	Cost/lb.	Weight	Cost/Apple
Smaller Apple	89¢		
Larger Apple	89¢		

Explain how you solved this problem: _____

_____

_____

_____

_____

_____

If the apples are on sale for 59¢ a pound, what does this do to the price for one apple? _____

_____

If a supermarket is having a sale on apples and sells them for 25¢ each, is that a good buy? Why or why not? _____

_____

_____

Buying Apples
by the Pound
Grading Matrix

Names _____

_____

_____

_____

Date _____   Class _____

Criteria	4	3	2	1
Quality of data collection				
Quality of problem-solving strategies				
Analysis and computation				
How well group worked together				

Comments:

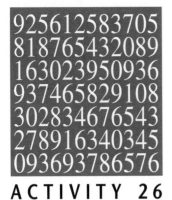

EggsCetera

MATH TOPICS

measurement (linear and mass), decimals, whole number operations, percent of difference, consumer pricing (best buy), estimation, circumference, formulas, mathematical vocabulary

---

TYPES OF INTELLIGENCES

logical/mathematical, bodily/kinesthetic, verbal/linguistic, interpersonal, visual/spatial, naturalist

---

CONCEPTS

Students will do the following:

1. Measure circumference of objects to the nearest mm and compare them

2. Determine the mass of objects and compare them

3. Problem solve to find the height of the eggs to the nearest mm

4. Find the difference of the measurements

5. Find the percent of difference of the measurements

6. Determine the relationship between the size of a product and its cost

MATERIALS

"EggsCetera" worksheets for each group of students; 1 medium, large, and jumbo hard-boiled egg for each group; 1 scale for each group; 1 tape measure with metric measurements for each group; rulers for each group; calculators; overhead transparency (worksheet 3) to find the average measurements and differences; prices of each egg size

WHAT TO DO

Students will work in groups of three to find the circumference, mass, and height of each of their eggs. The collected data is used to answer the questions on worksheet 2. To find the percent of increase (difference), the following formula is used: difference/original measurement x 100. Use the measurement of the smaller of the two eggs to find the percent of increase.

Hard boil enough eggs of each size so that each group will have one of each size. Supply student groups with the worksheets. Prepare an overhead transparency of worksheet 3 to find the average circumference, mass, and height of each of the sizes. These averages are used to compare the relationship that may or may not exist between the size of the egg and the price. For example: if medium eggs are selling for 69¢ a dozen, or 5.75¢ each, and large eggs are selling for 89¢ a dozen, or 7.4¢ each, the difference is 1.65¢. The ratio of increase to the cost of the medium eggs is 1.65¢/69¢, or .02 (.02 x 100 equals 2%). If the percent of difference in the size of the eggs is less than 2 percent, then buying the smaller egg is a better buy; if the percent of difference between the sizes is greater than 2 percent, then the larger egg is the better buy! By using average sizes, these computations can be performed by the entire class.

VARIATION

Have students find the better buy by researching small, medium, and large sizes of other products, such as detergents, cereals, milk, etc.

ASSESSMENT

1. Observation of student groups and worksheets

2. Grading matrix

3. Journal question: "If large eggs are selling for 79¢ a dozen and jumbo eggs are selling for $1.29 a dozen, how much more are you paying for each jumbo egg than each large egg? What percent of difference is this?"

EggsCetera
Worksheet 1

Names _____

Date _____   Class _____

Have you ever wondered why there are so many different sizes of eggs? Is one size a better buy than the others? Are jumbo eggs so much bigger than medium eggs that they are worth the increased price? What do you think?_____

How much bigger are they? _____

How much more do you think they weigh? _____

The experiment we will be conducting today will help us understand the differences in the sizes of eggs!

Directions: Working in groups of three, you will be taking three different measurements: (1) *Circumference.* The circumference is the distance around the egg at the widest point. Record each length in the space provided on your data collection table; (2) *Mass.* Be sure to record the mass in the correct place on the table; and (3) *Height.*

Cooperate to get the most accurate measurements possible!

Size of Egg	Circumference in cm	Mass in grams	Height in cm
Medium			
Large			
Jumbo			

EggsCetera
Worksheet 2

Names _____

Date _____   Class _____

Use the data you have collected to answer these questions:

Question	Difference	% of Difference
What is the difference between the circumference of the medium and the large egg?		
What is the difference between the circumference of the medium and the jumbo egg?		
What is the difference between the circumference of the large and the jumbo egg?		
What is the difference between the mass of the medium and the large egg?		
What is the difference between the mass of the medium and the jumbo egg?		
What is the difference between the mass of the large and the jumbo egg?		
What is the difference between the height of the medium and the large egg?		
What is the difference between the height of the medium and the jumbo egg?		
What is the difference between the height of the large and the jumbo egg?		

EggsCetera
Worksheet 3

Group	Circumference			Mass			Height		
	Medium	Large	Jumbo	Medium	Large	Jumbo	Medium	Large	Jumbo
1									
2									
3									
4									
5									
6									
7									
8									
9									
10									
Class Mean									

Something to think about . . . 1 doz. medium eggs cost 79¢

1 doz. large eggs cost 98¢

1 doz. jumbo eggs cost $1.09

What's the best buy? _____

EggsCetera
Grading Matrix

Names _____

_____

_____

_____

Date _____   Class _____

Criteria	4	3	2	1
Accuracy of group measurements				
Quality of data analysis				
Accuracy of computations				
How well group worked together				

Comments:

CHAPTER 5

Data Collection and Probability

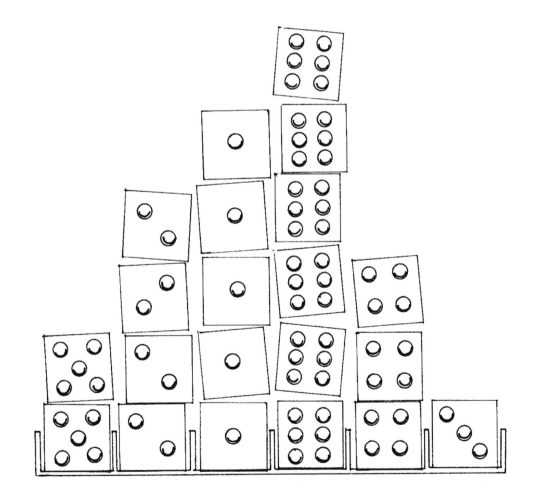

CHAPTER 5

Data Collection and Probability

We live in an age of technology where the information explosion requires us to not only understand how data is collected, but also how it is processed, translated into usable knowledge, and used to make predictions and decisions. John Allen Paulos (1988) maintains that the combination of our inability to deal with massive quantities of data and our misconceptions about the laws of probability have resulted in misinformed government policies and poorly planned personal decisions.

Statistical activities should develop students' appreciation of how data is used in the "real world." The process should take students through four processes:

- collection

- organization

- analysis

- graphic representation

Students should collect data to elicit relevant personal information. The investigation should help students better understand their world and themselves. Students should look for patterns or trends, and "what if" questions must be asked. Graphing the data allows students to present the data that has been sorted and classified and is a natural extension of the organization phase.

SUPER SURVEY

"Super Survey" is an open-ended problem that allows students to move through a complete data-collection activity. The students design a question that is of interest to them and then organize the responses in a frequency table. By computing the ratio and percent, students begin the process of analyzing their data. Finally, a graph is constructed and examined.

WHAT IS YOUR FAVORITE SUBJECT?

Some surveys require greater organization of the data for future analysis; "What Is Your Favorite Subject?" is an example of such a survey. Students do not give the participants choices, but rather allow for free response. These responses need to be categorized, grouped, and analyzed. Allowing students to make two different types of graphs encourages them to evaluate both in order to determine which better represents the data collected. Is one graph a better choice than the other? A good question to respond to in a journal question, perhaps.

ONE DIE AND PROBABILITY

While statistics and probability are grouped together, they are different concepts. Probability, or the measure of a likelihood of an event, can be determined either experimentally or theoretically. To comprehend theoretical probability, students must have activities and experiments that increase their understanding of what a 30-percent chance of rain means, or why a game is "fair" or "unfair." We can draw marbles out of a bag, spin dials, or roll dice to give students these necessary experiences. In this chapter there are three activities that build probability concepts. The first, "One Die and Probability," is an introductory activity that shows there is an equally likely probability, $1/6$, for each possible occurence, or event. Students are asked to design a circle graph of their results.

PAIR OF DICE AND PROBABILITY

"Pair of Dice and Probability" involves a more difficult concept. Students are required to compute the probability of an event by calculating all the possible outcomes of tossing a pair of dice. Although 2 + 5, 5 + 2, 4 + 3, and 3 + 4 have the same sum, they account for four different outcomes. By working together and discussing their findings, students develop their interpersonal intelligences while they increase their understanding of the mathematical concept of chance.

IS THIS GAME FAIR?

"Is This Game Fair?" asks students to predict if the game is fair, then gather necessary information to analyze and modify their original prediction on the basis of this new data. This type of activity is fundamental to developing higher-level reasoning. What is a fair game? Interesting discussions can be conducted in the mathematics classroom!

DINOSAURS AND PROBABILITY

"Probability theory is the underpinning of the modern world. Current research in both the physical and social sciences cannot be understood without it. Today's politics, tomorrow's weather report, and next week's satellites all depend on it" (Huff and Geise 1959).

"Dinosaurs and Probability" is an activity that encourages students to use prediction and communicates to students the power of mathematics. With this activity, the correctness of the students' answers is not immediately evident. Students need to gather additonal information to determine the validity of their original prediction.

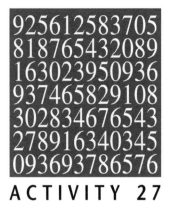

ACTIVITY 27

Super Survey

MATH TOPICS

data collection, organization, analysis, circle graphs, ratio, percent, use of protractor

---

TYPES OF INTELLIGENCES

verbal/linguistic, logical/mathematical, interpersonal, visual/spatial

---

CONCEPTS

Students will do the following:

1. Design a survey question including choices for response

2. Question thirty-six fellow students to collect data

3. Organize data on a frequency table

4. Compute frequency, ratio, percent, and degrees needed to produce a circle graph

5. Create a circle graph of the data

6. Analyze the graph

MATERIALS

"Super Survey" worksheets for each student; protractors; calculators; markers, crayons, or colored pencils; rulers

WHAT TO DO

Ask students, "Why do we take surveys? What characteristics of the questions and choices make the survey more accurate? Why must we think carefully about the choices we give the respondents?" It is important that students understand that the way they phrase the questions and choices can make the results more accurate.

Students will need a day to take the survey and enter their results on the table. The next day in class, give them protractors, rulers, and markers to design their graphs. Give students freedom to develop their own procedures to convert the percent (or number of people) to the necessary number of degrees in the angle of the circle graph. There are a number of ways they can solve this, and they should be given the opportunity to use the method that they "see"—the one that makes sense.

VARIATION

If you wish to simplify the activity, have students interview only twenty people. Cutting the number of responses makes it easier to find the percent and not too much more difficult to compute the number of degrees needed to draw the angle in the circle graph.

ASSESSMENT

1. Observation of students

2. Student products

3. Grading matrix

4. Journal question: "I am doing a survey and my question is, 'What is your favorite snake?' I am giving the respondent the following choices: garden snake, python, rattlesnake, spitting cobra. Do you think the quality of my choices are good or bad? Why?"

Super Survey
Worksheet 1

Name _____

Date _____   Class _____

You are going to conduct a survey. Choose a question carefully and write it out (in full) in the space provided below. It is important that you ask the question of each person in the same way, so do write it out. Choose four to six choices that you will give the respondents. List the choices below. Interview exactly thirty-six people.

My question: _____

My choices: _____

_____

_____

_____

_____

_____

_____

Choices	Tally	Frequency	Fraction $\frac{n}{36}$	Percent	Degrees of Circle $\frac{?}{360°}$

Super Survey
Worksheet 2

Name _____

Date _____   Class _____

Title: _____

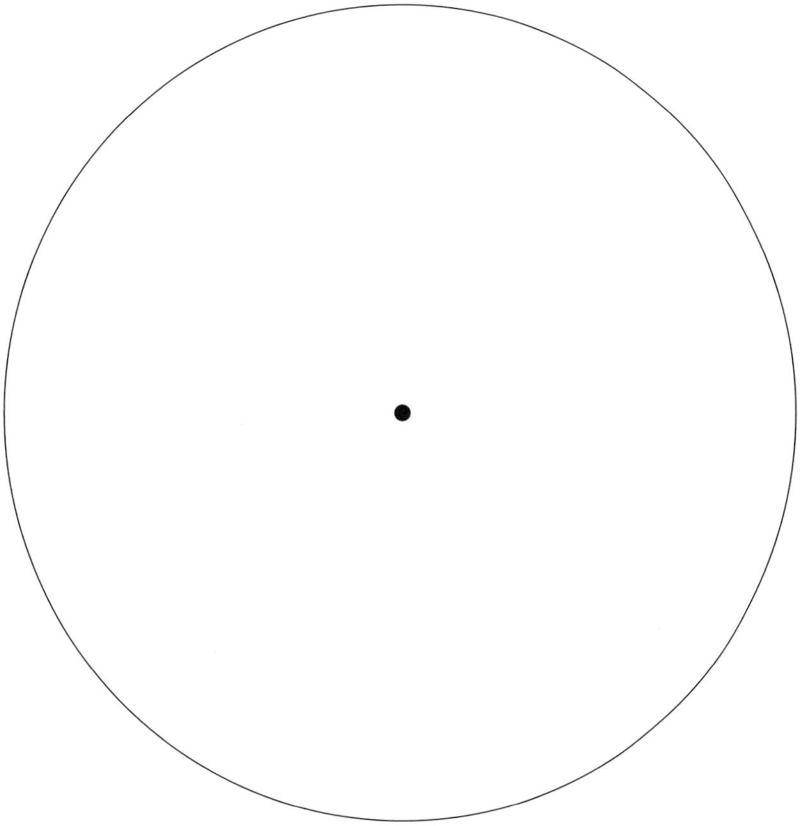

Describe some interesting facts about your data that is described in this graph. _____

_____

_____

_____

_____

_____

Super Survey
Grading Matrix

Name _____

Date _____ Class _____

Criteria	4	3	2	1
Wording of question				
Appropriateness of choices				
Accuracy of computation				
Quality of graph (angles accurate; titled and labeled correctly)				
Merit of analysis				
Comments:				

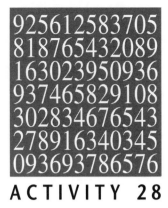

ACTIVITY 28

What Is Your Favorite Subject?

MATH TOPICS

data collection, organization, analysis, bar and circle graphs, use of protractors, percent

---

TYPES OF INTELLIGENCES

verbal/linguistic, logical/mathematical, visual/spatial, interpersonal, intrapersonal, naturalist

---

CONCEPTS

Students will do the following:

1. Collect nonstructured data

2. Organize the data into a frequency table

3. Graph the data using two different graphs

MATERIALS

worksheets 1, 2, and 3; protractors and rulers; colored pencils or markers

---

WHAT TO DO

Place students into groups of two and have them survey at least twenty students on what their favorite subject is. The responses and the sex of the respondents are recorded in the table provided. The data has to be organized on the frequency table. If the students wish to combine some subjects for ease of reporting, they must justify their decisions in their paragraphs. The results are reported by ratio and percent of girls and boys. Some attempt should be made to describe preference as a gender issue. The final step is graphing the results on a circle graph as well as a bar graph. The units for each should be designed by the students. You might request a separate graph from each student, thereby giving each student practice in determining units and making graphs.

VARIATION

Students can increase the number of variables by asking boys and girls in two or more grades. This makes the organization of the data more complicated, but it permits students to make comparisons between children of different ages.

ASSESSMENT

1. Observation of students

2. Student products on frequency table and graphs

3. Grading matrix

4. Journal question: "Describe the results of your survey and analyze any differences in the preferences of students (boys vs. girls, grade-level differences, etc.)."

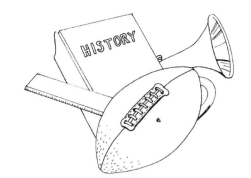

What Is Your Favorite Subject?
Worksheet 1

Names _____

Date _____ Class _____

My Favorite Subject—Data Collection

Name	Sex (Male or Female)	Subject

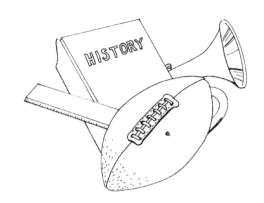

What Is Your Favorite Subject?
Worksheet 2

Names _____

Date _____   Class _____

Frequency Table of Results

Subject	# of Boys	# of Girls	Ratio of Boys	Ratio of Girls	% of Boys	% of Girls

What subject appeared to be the most popular with boys?_____

What subject appeared to be the most popular with girls? _____

You are writing an article for the school newspaper about your survey. The article should be a couple of paragraphs long and should be composed with well-written sentences.

What Is Your Favorite Subject?

Worksheet 3

Names _____

Date _____ Class _____

Bar Graph of Data

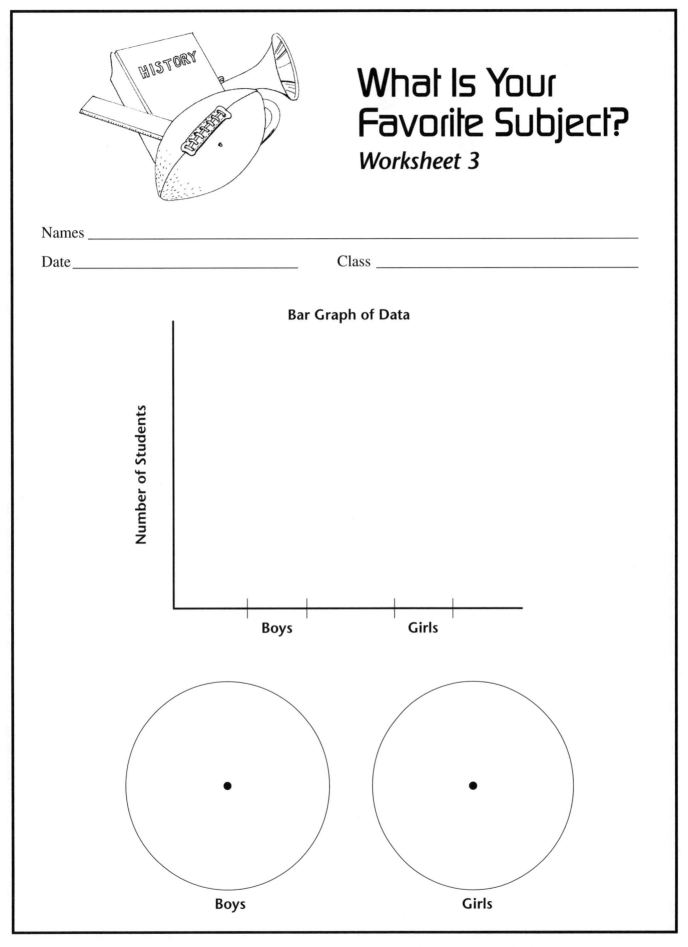

Number of Students

Boys   Girls

Boys   Girls

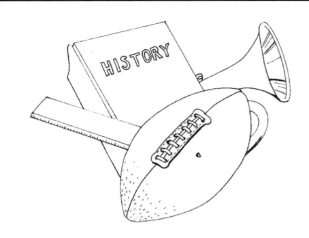

What Is Your Favorite Subject?
Grading Matrix

Names _____

_____

_____

_____

Date _____ Class _____

Criteria	4	3	2	1
Accuracy of data collection				
Quality of analysis of data				
Accuracy of computation				
Quality of circle graph (angles accurate; titled and labeled correctly)				
Quality of bar graph (units labeled correctly; measurement accurate)				
Comments:				

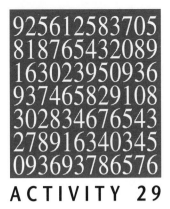

ACTIVITY 29

One Die
and Probability

MATH TOPICS

probability, data collection and analysis, fractions, percents, graphing

---

TYPES OF INTELLIGENCES

logical/mathematical, interpersonal, verbal/linguistic, visual/spatial, bodily/kinesthetic

---

CONCEPTS

Students will do the following:

1. Predict the outcome of a mathematical experiment

2. Work with a partner to conduct two experiments that use one die and a pair of dice

3. Collect class results to further analyze the data

4. Draw a pie chart of their results

MATERIALS

1 die for each pair of students; "One Die and Probability" worksheets for each pair of students

WHAT TO DO

Begin the discussion by asking students the following:

1. What possible numbers can appear when we roll one die?

2. Do you think that each of the numbers will appear the same number of times?

3. What do you think will happen if we roll one die one-hundred times?

If you wish, you can record the discussion on the blackboard or on newsprint. Students, working with a partner, continue working through the experiments. Your role is to act as a facilitator while the students collect their data. Since there is an equal chance of each occurrence, the graph should resemble the graph below.

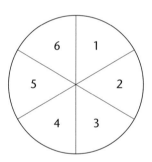

Have pairs of students divide the tasks: one student rolls the die while the other records the data. The final task for each pair is to answer the questions that are part of the lesson and draw a pie graph of their results.

VARIATION

Using one die, there is an equal probability of each occurrance. A spinner can be designed (similar to the graph shown above). Each of the central angles should measure 60°. When these two experiments are performed at the same time, students see the similarity between the methods and their resulting probability of $1/6$.

ASSESSMENT

1. Observation of student groups

2. Grading matrix

3. Journal question: "Explain why the probability of rolling a given number with one die is called 'equally likely.'"

One Die and Probability
Worksheet 1

Names _____

_____

Date _____   Class _____

Directions: You and your partner will be working on two different experiments with dice. Before rolling the dice, you will be asked to predict what will occur. Be sure to write down your predictions.

Experiment: Roll one die 100 times and record your results.

1. What are the possible things that can happen? _____

_____

2. What do you predict will happen? _____

_____

Now conduct the experiment. Record your results below.

# That Appears on Die	Tally	Frequency	Fraction	Percent
1				
2				
3				
4				
5				
6				
Total				

One Die and Probability

Worksheet 2

Names _____

_____

Date _____   Class _____

Draw a graph of your results in the circle provided. Be sure to label your sections.

Title of Graph _____

One Die and Probability
Grading Matrix

Names _____

_____

_____

_____

Date _____   Class _____

Criteria	4	3	2	1
Quality of data collection and computation				
Quality of analysis of experiment (including graph)				
How well pair worked together				

Comments:

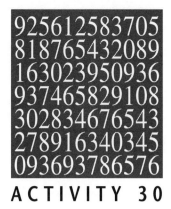

Pair of Dice and Probability

MATH TOPICS

probability, data collection and analysis, fractions, percents, graphing

---

TYPES OF INTELLIGENCE

logical/mathematical, interpersonal, verbal/linguistic, visual/spatial, bodily/kinesthetic

---

CONCEPTS

Students will do the following:

1. Predict the outcome of a mathematical experiment

2. Work with a partner to conduct the experiment and analyze the results

3. Collect class results to further analyze the data

4. Draw a bar graph of their results

MATERIALS

1 pair of dice for each pair of students; 1 set of "Pair of Dice and Probability" worksheets 1, 2, and 4 for each pair of students; overhead transparency of worksheet 3

WHAT TO DO

Begin the discussion by asking students the following:

1. "What possible sums can appear when we roll a pair of dice?"

2. "Do you think that each of the sums will appear the same number of times?"

3. "What do you think will happen if we roll the dice one hundred times?"

If you wish, you can record the discussion on the blackboard or on newsprint. Students, working with a partner, continue working through the experiment. Your role is to act as a facilitator while the students collect their data. When the data collection is complete, record the group data on worksheet 3 and work with students to find the means. The probability of each sum occurring relates to the number of possibilities each sum has to appear. A 6 x 6 matrix is a good way to show students all of the possible outcomes.

+	1	2	3	4	5	6
1	2	3	4	5	6	7
2	3	4	5	6	7	8
3	4	5	6	7	8	9
4	5	6	7	8	9	10
5	6	7	8	9	10	11
6	7	8	9	10	11	12

There is only one way to get a sum of 2; therefore, the probability of getting a sum of 2 is 1 out of 36, or $\frac{1}{36}$; three is $\frac{2}{36}$; etc. Students can use ratio/proportion to figure out the theoretical probability of an event occurring. For example, the probability of a sum of 7 occurring is $\frac{1}{6}$; so if the dice are tossed 100 times, the ratio would be $\frac{1}{6} = \frac{X}{100}$, or about 17 occurrences. The bar graph will resemble the following graph.

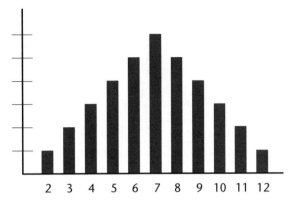

Have pairs of students divide up the tasks: one student rolls the dice while the other records the data. When they have collected their data, it is placed on worksheet 3 for further analysis. The final task for each pair is to answer the questions that are part of the lesson and draw a bar graph of their results.

VARIATION

This experiment is well suited for grades seven and eight. The problem solving necessary to find theoretical probability is the same strategy required for the "Is This Game Fair?" activity.

ASSESSMENT

1. Observation of student groups (use group checklist)

2. Grading matrix

3. Journal question: "Do you believe, based on the results of your experiment, that there is an 'equally likely' probability that each sum will appear?"

Pair of Dice and Probability
Worksheet 1

Names _____

_____

Date _____   Class _____

Directions: You and your partner will be working on two different experiments with a pair of dice. Before rolling the dice, you will be asked to predict what you think will occur. Be sure to write down your predictions.

Experiment: Roll a pair of dice 100 times, find the sum, and record your results.

1. What are the possible things that can happen? _____

_____

2. What do you predict will happen? Do you think one sum will appear more often than another? Why?

_____

Now conduct the experiment. Record your results below.

Sum of the dice	Tally	Frequency	Fraction	Percent
2				
3				
4				
5				
6				
7				
8				
9				
10				
11				
12				
Total				

Explain your results _____

_____

Pair of Dice and Probability

Worksheet 2

Names _____

_____

Date _____   Class _____

Directions: Create a graph of the data you collected during your experiment. Be sure to label each axis correctly.

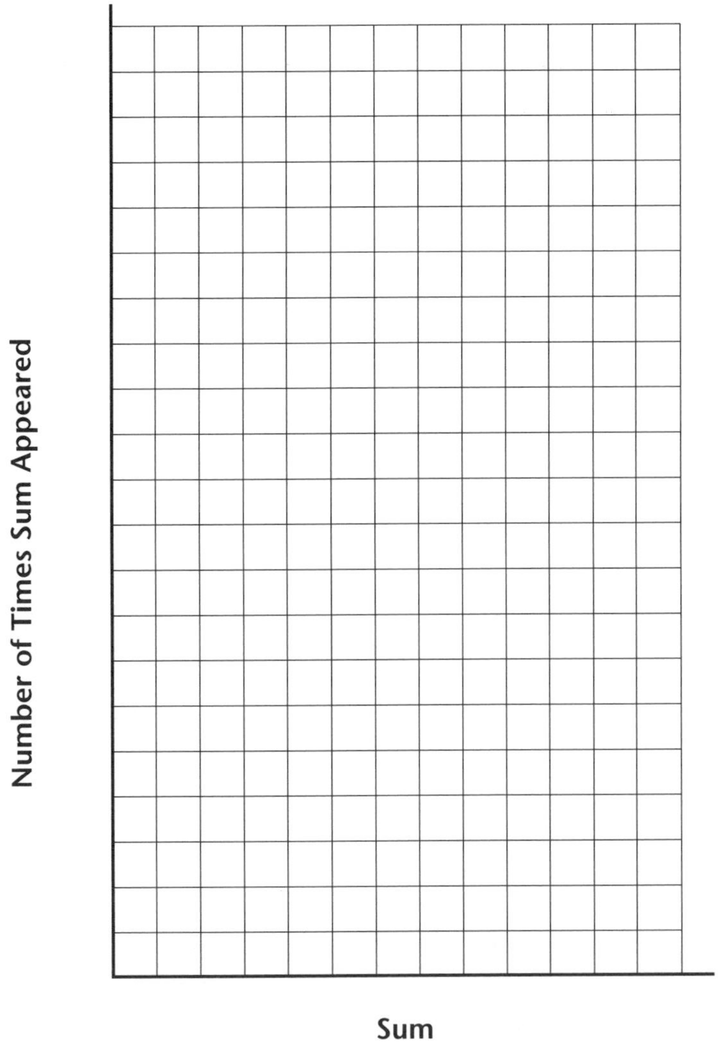

Number of Times Sum Appeared

Sum

Pair of Dice and Probability
Worksheet 3

Class Data

Record the number of times each of these sums appeared in your data.

Pair	Sum of										
	2	3	4	5	6	7	8	9	10	11	12
A											
B											
C											
D											
E											
F											
G											
H											
I											
J											
K											
L											
M											
N											
O											
Means											

Pair of Dice and Probability
Worksheet 4

Names _____

_____

Date _____   Class _____

Work with your partner to analyze the "Pair of Dice and Probability" experiment by answering these questions:

1. Does it appear that one sum occurs more often than others? Explain your answer.

   _____

   _____

   _____

   _____

2. Why do you think you got the results you did? Consider the different ways each of the sums can appear; for example, how many different ways can you obtain a sum of 2? A sum of 9? Which sum has the greatest chance because it has the largest number of combinations?

   _____

   _____

   _____

   _____

3. Explain the difference in probability and chance when you roll a pair of dice instead of just one die. _____

   _____

   _____

   _____

Pair of Dice and Probability
Grading Matrix

Names _____

_____

_____

_____

Date _____   Class _____

Criteria	4	3	2	1
Quality of data collection and computation				
Quality of analysis of experiment				
Quality of graph				
How well pair worked together				
Comments:				

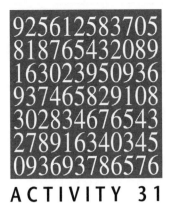

ACTIVITY 31

Is This Game Fair?

MATH TOPICS

probability, odds, data collection and analysis, problem solving

---

TYPES OF INTELLIGENCES

logical/mathematical, interpersonal, intrapersonal, visual/spatial, bodily/kinesthetic

---

CONCEPT

Students will do the following:

1. Analyze the concept of "fairness"

2. Predict whether or not a game is fair based on the payoff

3. Collect the necessary data to analyze their predictions and make corrections if necessary

4. Analyze the odds to determine how to make the game fair

MATERIALS

1 pair of dice for each pair of students; copies of "Is This Game Fair?" worksheets; overhead transparency of worksheet 2

WHAT TO DO

Begin discussion by passing out game sheets and reading the directions with the students. Allow students time to discuss whether or not they believe the game is fair. Bring the discussion around to the idea of fairness and what makes a game fair. Is it fair if you win? Does fair mean there is an equal chance of either player winning?

Once students have made their predictions, allow them time to play the game. The original sheet allows for two games to be played; each member of the group has a chance to be the player once and the banker once. If there is additional time, use the second sheet provided. When all groups are finished, record their results on the "Class Record" table for ease of analysis. The more games that are played, the better chance that theoretical odds will be obtained. Since the probability of rolling a double is $1/6$ $(6/36)$, the odds are that five times the player will roll other than a double and one time the face will be a double. Ask the students to devise a game that is "fair." One of the ways the game can be made fair is by having the banker pay the player $5 for each double rolled.

Students begin by making their predictions and then, working in pairs, play the maximum number of games they can in the time provided. After playing the game, pairs of students should analyze their predictions and make corrections, if necessary, based on their results. Each pair must determine how they would change the rules to make this game fair.

VARIATION

This activity is designed for students who have had some experience with probability and odds. It is best to give fifth and sixth grade students experiences rolling one die, spinning dials, tossing coins, etc.

ASSESSMENT

1. Observation of student pairs

2. Grading matrix

3. Journal question: "We are going to change the rules of the game as follows: The player wins if the sum on the dice is a multiple of three. What payoff would make this new game fair?"

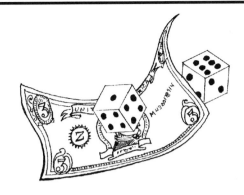

Is This Game Fair?
Worksheet 1

Names _____

Date _____   Class _____

Directions: For this game there will be a "player" and a "banker." Each will start out with $10.00. The object of the game is to see who can win the most amount of money. Use the tables below to play the game using these rules:

1. Only the player rolls the dice. (You will take turns taking the role of player.)

2. The dice are tossed and the sum of the two faces is taken.

3. If the player rolls a double, the banker must pay the player $3.00.

4. If the player rolls other than a double, the player pays the banker only $1.00.

Do you think this game is fair? Why or why not? _____

_____

_____

Now play the game with your partner. Take turns being the "player" or the "banker." Play as many games as you can during the time allotted. When you have finished, reevaluate your original prediction as to the "fairness" of this game.

	Did the player roll a double?									
	Starts with	Yes or No?	Yes or No?	Yes or No?	Yes or No?	Yes or No?	Yes or No?	Yes or No?	Yes or No?	Yes or No?	Yes or No?
Player	$10										
Banker	$10										

	Did the player roll a double?									
	Starts with	Yes or No?	Yes or No?	Yes or No?	Yes or No?	Yes or No?	Yes or No?	Yes or No?	Yes or No?	Yes or No?	Yes or No?
Player	$10										
Banker	$10										

Is This Game Fair?—Worksheet 1 (Continued)

		Did the player roll a double?									
	Starts with	Yes or No?	Yes or No?	Yes or No?	Yes or No?	Yes or No?	Yes or No?	Yes or No?	Yes or No?	Yes or No?	Yes or No?
Player	$10										
Banker	$10										

		Did the player roll a double?									
	Starts with	Yes or No?	Yes or No?	Yes or No?	Yes or No?	Yes or No?	Yes or No?	Yes or No?	Yes or No?	Yes or No?	Yes or No?
Player	$10										
Banker	$10										

		Did the player roll a double?									
	Starts with	Yes or No?	Yes or No?	Yes or No?	Yes or No?	Yes or No?	Yes or No?	Yes or No?	Yes or No?	Yes or No?	Yes or No?
Player	$10										
Banker	$10										

		Did the player roll a double?									
	Starts with	Yes or No?	Yes or No?	Yes or No?	Yes or No?	Yes or No?	Yes or No?	Yes or No?	Yes or No?	Yes or No?	Yes or No?
Player	$10										
Banker	$10										

		Did the player roll a double?									
	Starts with	Yes or No?	Yes or No?	Yes or No?	Yes or No?	Yes or No?	Yes or No?	Yes or No?	Yes or No?	Yes or No?	Yes or No?
Player	$10										
Banker	$10										

How many times did the banker win? _____

How many times did the player win? _____

Do you think the game is fair after playing these games? Explain your reasoning. _____

_____

_____

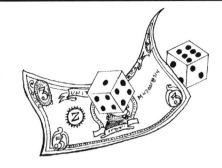

Is This Game Fair?
Worksheet 2

Names _____

Date _____ Class _____

Class Record

Group Number	Number of Times the Banker Won	Number of Times the Player Won
1		
2		
3		
4		
5		
6		
7		
8		
9		
10		
11		
12		
13		
14		
15		
Total		

Now that we have additional data, does it appear that this game is fair? _____

_____

If you do not think it is fair, how do you think we could change the rules to make it fair? _____

_____

_____

Is This Game Fair?

Worksheet 3

Names _____

Date _____ Class _____

Written Analysis

What were the results of the games you played? Be as specific as you can in your descriptions.

_____

_____

Did you initially believe the game was fair? Why did you believe that? _____

_____

Do you still hold that opinion? Why or why not? _____

_____

After analyzing what happened, what do you think could be done to these rules to make this game more fair? _____

_____

_____

_____

_____

Work with your partner to design a game, using the sum that appears on a pair of dice. Be sure to make the game a fair game. Tell why your game is fair. _____

_____

_____

_____

_____

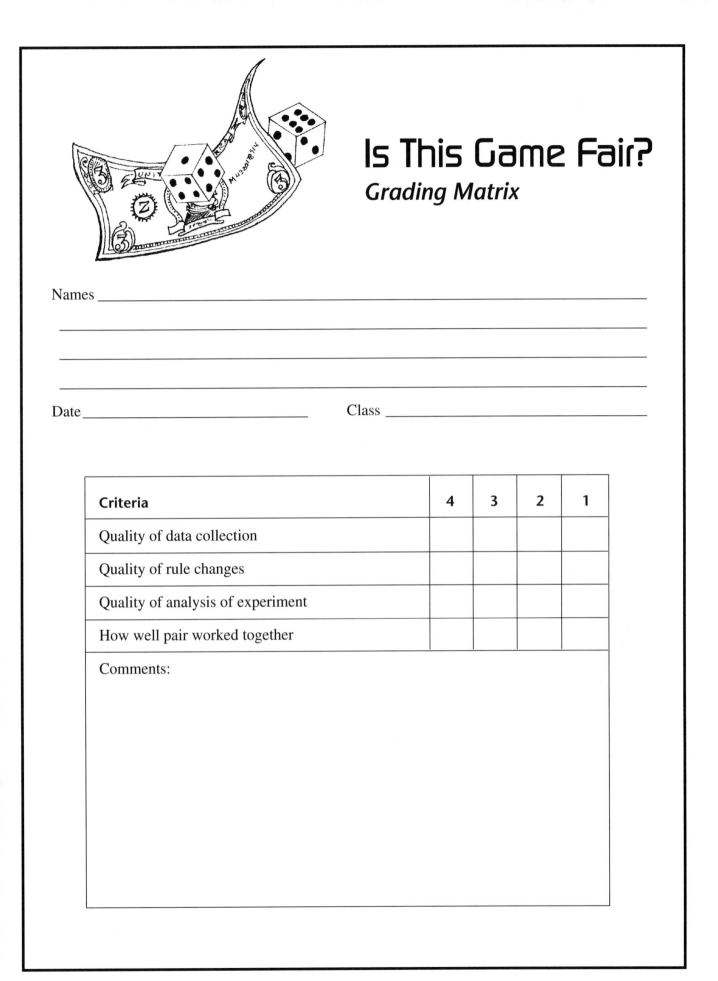

Is This Game Fair?
Grading Matrix

Names _____

_____

_____

_____

Date _____ Class _____

Criteria	4	3	2	1
Quality of data collection				
Quality of rule changes				
Quality of analysis of experiment				
How well pair worked together				
Comments:				

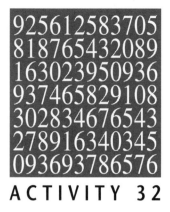

Dinosaurs and Probability

MATH TOPICS

probability, ratio and proportion, data analysis, rounding

TYPES OF INTELLIGENCES

visual/spatial, logical/mathematical, verbal/linguistic, interpersonal, bodily/kinesthetic

---

CONCEPTS

Students will do the following:

1. Make a prediction based on their analysis of an experiment

2. Work collaboratively with a classmate to conduct an experiment

3. Use ratio and proportion to problem solve

MATERIALS

dinosaurs in green, yellow, orange, red, purple, blue (Plastic dinosaurs can be purchased in most school supply catalogs. If dinosaurs are not available, a sheet has been provided that can be duplicated on heavy stock in the recommended colors. They can then be cut out for use in the experiment.); paper lunch bags; calculators; "Dinosaurs and Probability" worksheet for each pair of students

---

WHAT TO DO

Discuss with the students whether they can predict the colors of the dinosaurs in their bags without looking. They should know the following: (1) there are twelve dinosaurs of varying colors in each bag, (2) they are not to peek in their bags, and (3) after they draw a dinosaur out, they are to tally it on their data collection sheet and then return it to the bag.

The mathematics behind this lesson: let's suppose that blue dinosaurs were drawn out of the bag 8 times. Students can set up the following ratio $\frac{8}{36} = \frac{n}{12}$. Using proportions, we can compute that n = $2\frac{2}{3}$ which rounds to 3. Our prediction would be that there are between 2 and 3 blue dinosaurs in the bag—most probably 3.

VARIATION

This activity works well for all grade levels. The more trials that are performed, the better the prediction should be.

ASSESSMENT

1. Observation of student groups

2. Grading matrix

3. Student products

4. Journal question: "Explain how you used ratio and proportion to predict the number of each color of dinosaur in your bag."

Dinosaurs and Probability

Worksheet 1

Names _____

Date _____

Class _____

Do you think you can predict how many of each color of dinosaurs there are in a paper bag without looking? This experiment will see if you can do just that.

Directions: Twelve randomly colored dinosaurs have been placed into each paper lunch bag. With your partner, draw one dinosaur from the bag and record its color on the table below. Be sure not to look into the bag. Use tally marks to record each pick, then return the dinosaur to the bag and shake it up. Draw another dinosaur and record the color of the second one. Do this a total of thirty-six times. Use your results to predict how many of each of the colors appear in the bag.

Color	Tally	Ratio $\frac{n}{36}$	Proportion $\frac{n}{36} = \frac{d}{12}$	Mixed Number	Rounded Prediction
Green					
Yellow					
Red					
Orange					
Purple					
Blue					
Totals					

Were your predictions close? _____

Why do you think you got the results you did?_____

If you are not satisfied with your results, how do you think you could alter the experiment to have more accurate results?_____

_____

_____

_____

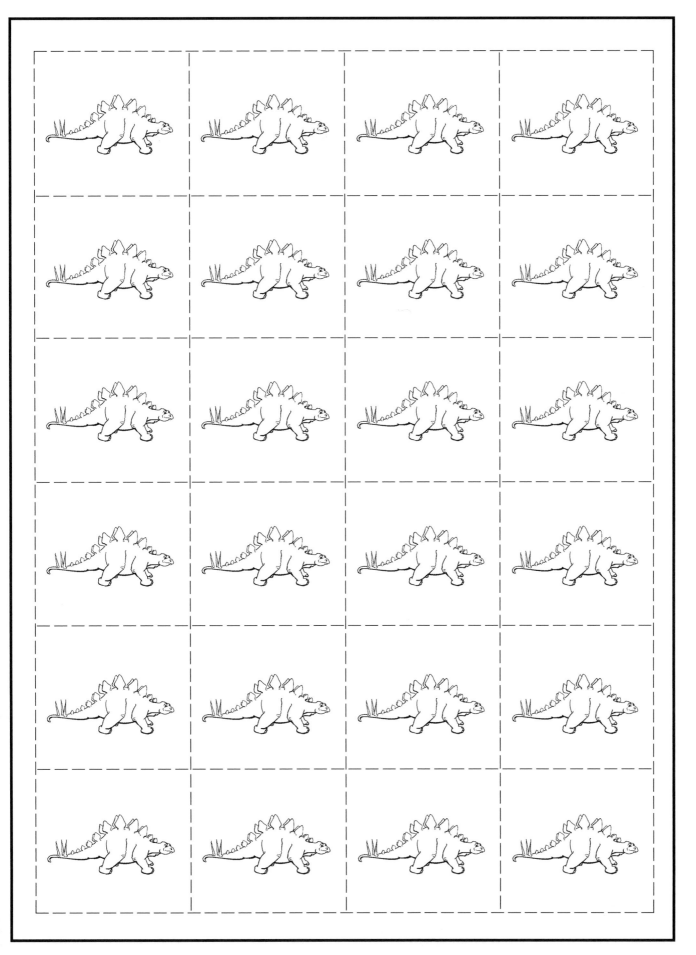

Dinosaurs
and Probability
Grading Matrix

Names _____

_____

_____

_____

Date _____   Class _____

Criteria	4	3	2	1
Quality of data collection				
Quality of analysis (accuracy of predictions)				
How well pair worked together				
Comments:				

Appendix
Designing Your Own Activities

The first step to designing your own activities is to think of a problem or question that you or your students would like to find the answer to. For example: How many basketballs could we fit in the classroom? How many different ways can we form a magic square using the numbers 1 through 9? How high would a stack of 1,000,000 pennies reach? What is the favorite color of sixth grade students?

Once you've decided on a question to address, mentally work through an activity related to the question. Will you need data collection sheets? Will students require a frequency table? Do you want students to work in pairs or in groups of three or four? The following steps will help you design your own activity:

1. Design the sheets your students will use to complete the activity.

2. Examine the activity carefully and see how it fits into and enhances your mathematics curriculum. Using the "Teacher's Page" template, list the math strands next to "Math Topics."

3. Remember to keep in mind the multiple intelligences. What type of activities will the students be doing? Will they be working together? Will they be explaining their reasoning in journal or written form? Carefully examine the activity to find the intelligences that will be used. List these next to "Types of Intelligences" on the template.

4. What skills and concepts will students be exposed to in this activity? Work through these carefully, as you will need them to tie your instruction to your assessment and evaluation. Describe the skills and concepts next to "Concepts."

5. In your mind's eye, go through the activity. What materials will your students need to complete it? What will you need? Consider overhead transparencies, copies of the worksheets for the students, rulers, calculators, crayons, markers, etc. Be thorough! There's nothing worse than needing something and having a room full of scholars waiting to get started! List the necessary supplies next to "Materials."

6. To facilitate the lesson, I always begin with a question for the students. By using a question to open the lesson, I am able to make it seem more like an exploration rather than an exercise. Be careful; you want to give the students enough information to get started, but not so much that the creativity of inquiry is lost! This is a delicate balance. I can say from experience that a good teacher will constantly reevaluate and reconsider his or her options. Just remember: When you tell a child how to solve a problem, you are imparting your method of solution using the intelligence that you are most comfortable with. Plan a beginning (the initial question or statement of the problem), a middle (time for the students to work through the activity), and a conclusion. The conclusion may involve bringing the class together to find an average or mean (design a chart to collect the data); or, you might want to have a class discussion of the results (give each group the opportunity to explain not only their answer, but the methods they used to solve the problem). In any case the lesson needs to be tied together. As the facilitator, you need to bring closure. Write how you will do this next to "What to Do" on the "Teacher's Page."

7. "Variation" is your opportunity to design additional extension activities to better meet the needs of our diverse student populations. If a group finishes before others, is there an extension activity that is more than "busy work"? Are there students who would benefit from a more detailed project? You might need to work through

the original activity once before these variations become obvious.

8. Tying instruction to assessment and evaluation is a critical component of activity-based mathematics. The template for the "Teacher's Page" lists observation of students, student products, grading matrix, other, and journal question(s). Let's examine each of these individually.

   a. Observation of Students: This can be done either informally or by using the observation sheets supplied. It is important that students be evaluated in a formal way at least once or twice during each grading period.

   b. Student Products: Did you design a data collection sheet for the students? This, along with other materials the students complete for the activity, can be used as part of the assessment and evaluation process.

   c. Grading Matrix: A template of a grading matrix has been supplied. It is designed to accommodate four skills and/or concepts that you have previously outlined. Consider what you want your students to know or to have accomplished once they have completed the activity. Use these as criteria on the grading matrix.

   d. Other: Is there something you would like to use as another form of evaluation? Have you designed a test or quiz? Does your activity parallel a textbook problem that you would like to use? Tailor your assessment to your own classroom needs.

   e. Journal Question(s): This will give your students the opportunity to explain, in their own words, an important concept of the lesson, how they solved a particular problem, or how well they understand a skill. It is important that the question be more open ended and more than merely right or wrong. You might want to grade it on a five-point scale based upon the accuracy and completeness of the response.

Plunge right in! It's easier than it appears and a lot more exciting than following the pages of the textbook for the entire school year!

Template of
Teacher's Page

MATH TOPICS

TYPES OF INTELLIGENCES

CONCEPTS

MATERIALS

WHAT TO DO

VARIATION

ASSESSMENT

1. Observation of students

2. Student products

3. Grading matrix

4. Other

5. Journal question(s):

Template of Grading Matrix

Names _____

_____

_____

_____

Date _____ Class _____

Criteria	4	3	2	1
Comments:				

Bibliography

Armstrong, T. 1993. *Seven kinds of smart.* New York: Penguin Books.

Chapman, C. 1993. *If the shoe fits . . . : How to develop multiple intelligences in the classroom.* Palatine, Ill.: IRI/Skylight Training and Publishing, Inc.

Chapman-Fahey, M. 1993. *Quilt-it bee math?* Presented at NCTM Regional Conference, Paducah, Ky.

Fuys, D., D. Geddes, and R. Tischler. 1988. *The van Hiele model of thinking in geometry among adolescents* in JRME monograph number 3. Reston, Va.: NCTM.

Gardner, H. 1985. *Frames of mind.* New York: Basic Books.

———. 1993. *Multiple intelligences: The theory in practice.* New York: Basic Books.

———. 1995. Reflections on multiple intelligences: Myths and messages. *Phi Delta Kappan,* November, 200–209.

Huff, D., and Greiss. 1959. *How to take a chance.* New York: W.W. Norton & Co.

Martin, H. 1991. Is this game fair? In *Dealing with data and chance,* edited by J. S. Zawojewski. Reston, Va.: NCTM.

Mathematical Sciences Education Board, National Research Council. 1989. *Everybody counts: A report to the nation on the future of mathematics education.* Washington, D.C.: National Academy Press.

———. 1993. *Measuring what counts: A conceptual guide for mathematics assessment.* Washington, D.C.: National Academy Press.

National Association of Educational Progress (NAEP). 1979, October. NAEP Newsletter.

National Council of Teachers of Mathematics (NCTM). 1989. *Curriculum and evaluation standards for school mathematics.* Reston, Va.: NCTM.

———. 1991. *Professional standards for teaching mathematics.* Reston, Va.: NCTM.

———. 1995. *Assessment standards for school mathematics.* Reston, Va.: NCTM.

Paulos, J. A. 1988. *Innumeracy: Mathematical illiteracy and its consequences.* New York: Hill and Wang.

Sobel, M. A., and E. M. Maletsky. 1988. *Teaching mathematics.* Englewood Cliffs, N.J.: Prentice-Hall

Stenmark, J. K. 1989. *Assessment alternatives in mathematics.* Berkeley, Calif.: EQUALS, University of California.

Willoughby, S. S. 1990. *Mathematics education in a changing world.* Alexandria, Va.: ASCD.

There are

one-story intellects,

two-story intellects, and three-story

intellects with skylights. All fact collectors, who

have no aim beyond their facts, are one-story men. Two-story men

compare, reason, generalize, using the labors of the fact collectors as

well as their own. Three-story men idealize, imagine,

predict—their best illumination comes from

above, through the skylight.

—Oliver Wendell

Holmes

SkyLight
TRAINING AND PUBLISHING, INC.